SOCIETY
IN THE
ATHARVAVEDA

Reconstructing Indian History & Culture, no. 15

SOCIETY IN THE ATHARVAVEDA

B.S. Kharade

PRINTWORLD
Publishers of Indian Traditions

Cataloging in Publication Data--DK
[Courtesy: D.K. Agencies (P) Ltd. <docinfo@dkagencies.com>]

Kharade, B.S., author.
Society in the Atharvaveda / B.S. Kharade.
pages cm. – (Reconstructing Indian history & culture ; no. 15)
Includes passages in Sanskrit (Latin).
"First published in India in 1997" – Title page verso.
Includes bibliographical references and index.
ISBN 9788124600931 (Hb)

1. Vedas. Atharvaveda. – Criticism, interpretation, etc. 2. India – Social life and customs – To 1200. 3. India – Social conditions – To 1200. 4. Society in literature. I. Title. II. Series: Reconstructing Indian history & culture ; no. 15.

LCC BL1114.67.K43 2026 | DDC 294.59215046 23

ISBN 978-81-246-0093-1
First published in India in 1997
Reprinted in 2026

Printed and published by:
D.K. Printworld (P) Ltd.
Regd. Office: "Vedaśrī", F-395, Sudarshan Park
ESI Hospital Metro Station, New Delhi - 110015
Phones: (011) 4172 2626, 98713 94815
e-mail: indology@dkprintworld.com
Website: www.dkprintworld.com

Dedicated to the
ancient Indian scholar-agriculturist
and to all those who helped me
in writing this book

The *Atharvaveda* is a Vedic holy book — *Pothī* — that deals with the life of the common man in the ancient Indian community comprising the farmer, his wife, or rather, the village community as a whole of the time. It thus represents the life-history of the masses in ancient India; the rest of the Vedic literature may be considered as pertaining to a very small percentage (approximately ten per cent) of the ancient Indian community!

Preface

THE *Vedas* are together a bounty of intense and meaningful observations, gems of thought that are as profoundly significant today as they were in times of yore. These ancient texts of Indian heritage have a significance that well extends beyond the religious and philosoplhical contexts for there is a vast range of areas on which they shed light. One of their most valuable contributions has to do with the evolution of society: there are a number of references in the Vedic texts that taken together depict the life and times of the people at large. It is here that the *Atharvaveda* is of the greatest importance, for it is essentially the *Veda* concerned with the life of the common people.

The *Atharvaveda*, referred to as the fourth *Veda*, is said to be a later addition to the '*Vedatrayī*' — the *Ṛg, Sāma* and *Yajur Vedas*. Its 731 hymns hardly resembles those in the '*Vedatrayī*'. Unlike these three *Vedas*, the *Atharvaveda* is largely concerned with knowledge of ghosts, gnomes and magical formulae. All these factors have had their share in contributing to the subordination of this *Veda* to the others. Most of all, it may be because the *Atharvaveda* concerns itself with the ways and customs of common man — the ordinary village farmer, craftsman and others, and their families. But I believe that it is this factor in particular that accentuates the importance of this Vedic *pothī*, and so, my attempt there has been to lay bare various aspects of society in the Atharvavedic time as reflected in the *Atharvaveda* that deals with even the minutest of details with gravity.

In this book, I have dealt with a range of areas: the Atharvavedic people's technique of farming and breeding cattle; the village artisans specialised in various crafts; trade at the time and travel means and routes, the various tribes/peoples that interacted with each other in society; political administration; daily preoccupations and fashions of the layman and his wife; bad practices such as gambling and adultery; and so on. I have undertaken a brief and interesting discussion to show how this Vedic text is truly the foundation of source of many traditional folk songs that are sung even today by the common man at work in the villages. A chapter is given to analyse the status and role of women as apparent in the Atharvavedic verses. The last chapter discusses how the people of the *AV* time viewed and responded to their environment — an area which has emerged as a field of specialised study in recent years.

Modern scholarship has largely focused on the '*Vedatrayī*' and writings on the *Atharvaveda* are few. Modern scholars' interpretation of the *AV* is clearly from a perspective which is the traditional mode of interpreting the *AV*. I believe that it is high time scholars study the *Atharvaveda* for what it really is — a wealth of information about the life of the people at large, the masses — and accord due status to it. My work is a humble effort in that direction.

In course of writing this book, I was aided by many persons who extended to me persistent guidance and warm encouragement. I would like to mention, in particular, Dr. V.B. Inamadar, Professor in Sanskrit and Sanskrit-Pandit (Maharashtra-state) whose kind guidance and blessings encouraged me to write this book. I owe a deep sense of gratitude to my path-maker and guide, Dr. A.H. Salunkhe, Dean, Arts Faculty, Shivaji University, Kolhapur, Maharashtra and late Shri S.V. Kukarni who is responsible for strengthening my foundations in Sanskrit studies. I am thankful and highly indebted to my family members and relatives for their unmatchable support and patience while I was preoccupied with this work. I would also like to thank D.K. Printworld (P) Ltd. for their keen interest in publishing this work.

Satara **B.S. Kharade**

Contents

Abbreviations

AV	*Atharvaveda.*
ṚV	*Ṛgveda.*
SV	*Sāmaveda.*
YV	*Yajurveda.*
P.	Page.
PP.	Pages.
e.g.	For example.
i.e.	That is.
Vol.	Volume.

Transliteration Chart

	Vertical stroke above the letter to direct *svarita*. Pronounce with middle pitch.
	Horizontal stroke below the letter to direct *anudātta*. Pronounce with low pitch.
	No stroke to the letters from the verses to direct *udātta*. Pronounce with high pitch.
1	*Jātya-svarita* on short vowel.
3	*Jātya-svarita* on long vowel.
S	Dvikhaṇḍa or *avagraha*.
:	*Visarga* for *ḥ* or sign for half the stop.
˙	*Anusvāra* for *ṅ, ṃ, m̐, ṇ, ñ, m*.
—	Dash.
c	To pronounce as *ch* from 'church'.
ch	To pronounce as *chh* with proper pressure.
ṭ	To pronounce as *t* from 'tooth'.
ṭh	To pronounce *th* from 'tooth' with proper pressure.
ś	For *sh* from 'shirt'.
s	For *sh* but after touching the tongue backward than'ś'.
n	Like *n* from 'north'.

ṇ	nasal but with the tongue touching possibly backward.
l	*l* from 'school'.
ḷ	In Vedic Sanskrit and Marāṭhī as from *Mīḷhuṣe*.
a, i	Short vowels.
ā, ī	Long vowels.
ḍ	As *d* from 'code'.
ḍh	With proper pressure.

1

Introduction

THE *Atharvaveda*, the *Veda* bearing the names of the great worshippers of Agni, Atharvan and Aṅgiras is the *Veda* of the masses. It can be argued that the *AV* actually represents the life of the ancient Indian agriculturist community, that is the agriculturist himself and his fellowmen in the village together constituting the masses. Excavations in the past by Indian archaeologists in collaboration with their western counterparts in the central and southern regions of India have yielded a hoard of remains pertaining to some ancient agriculturist and cattle-breeding communities.[1] The details of the remains bear resemblances to what is found narrated in the *AV*. Moreover, scientific analysis especially of the clay and ashes from the sites have dated these remains to *c*. 2500-600 BC which is approximately the period of the *AV* of the neolithic age. Thanks to the archaeological findings, we can now rely on something more than literary evidence to sketch a picture of the life of the ancient farmer-community in India.

A word or two about this Vedic text, the *Atharvaveda* itself and a general sketch of the life of the common man as culled from this text is necessary before we delve into a deeper issue — that of the subordinate status of the *Atharvaveda* among the Vedic texts.

The Atharvaveda

The *AV* is found referred to by many titles such as *Ātharvaṇoveda*, *Āṅgiroveda*, *Āṅgirasīvidyā*, *Atharvaṅgīrasaḥ*. *Brahmaveda* and *Kṣātraveda*.

The *śākhās*, meaning branches or recensions, of the *AV* have two roots and each of these have nine recensions which comprise on the one hand, Paippala, Dānta, etc. and on the other, Paippalāda, Taudāyana, etc. However, of these, only two, Paippalāda and Śaunakīya, with their respective texts remain. Besides the *Brāhmaṇa, Śrauta* and *Gṛhyasūtra* texts, to this *Veda* belongs the supplementary *Kalpa-sūtra* texts, *Śānti, Nakṣatra* and *Āṅgirasa*. More than thirty *Upaniṣads* are attached to it but no *Āraṇyaka* text. It is the *Śaunakīya-saṃhitā* of *AV* which is seen as displaying fine editorial work. It is divided into 20 *kāṇḍas* or books with 731 hymns containing about 6000 verses. The books are arranged subjectwise as follows: (1) charms to cure diseases and possession by demons (*bhaiṣajyāni*), (2) prayers for the long life and health (*āyuṣyāni*), (3) imprecations against demons, sorcerers and enemies (*ābhicārikāṇi* and *kṛtyā-pratiharaṇāni*), (4) charms pertaining to women (*strīkarmāṇi*), (5) charms to secure harmony, influence in the assembly and the like (*sāṃmanasyāni*), (6) charms pertaining to royalty *(rājakarmāṇi)*, (7) prayers and imprecations in the interest of Brāhmaṇas, (8) charms to secure prosperity and freedom from danger (*pauṣṭikāni*), (9) charms in expiation of sin and defilement (*prāyaścittāni*), (10) cosmogonic and theosophic hymns, (11) ritualistic and general hymns, (12) the books dealing with individual themes like marriage, funeral rites, etc., (13) the twentieth book, and (14) the *Kuntāpa* hymns.

The Vedic scholars are of the view that the *AV* originated from two kinds of seers, viz., the Ātharvaṇa as 'Śānta' associated with holy magic to promote happiness and the Aṅgiras as 'Ghora' associated with hostile magic or black magic. It is owing to this twofold magic that the Vedic schools have identified the *AV* verses as possessing the power 'to bless, to appease and to curse'. Legendary accounts have also been attached to the *AV* in order to admit it into the group of the *Vedatrayī*. But these legends have no textual evidence to bear them out. It is more sensible to consider this text as 'man-made' especially as it mainly deals with secular themes. Further, it may be stated confidently that the seers who contributed the *AV* hymns in the *Saṃhitā* breathed and lived in this very world![2]

As far as the Atharvavedic society is concerned, there are a number of references in the Vedic text that, directly or indirectly, shed light on this aspect. We are informed, for instance, of a two-fold establishment, the colony of Āryans and that of Śūdras, and this may be a description of the society at the time.

> *udágrabhaṃ parıpāṇádyātụdhānáṃ kimīdinám* ।
> *tenāhaṃ sarváṃ paśyāmyụta Śūdramụtāryám* ।।
>
> Please arise and protect us from the magician and robber to let me see who is the Śūdra and who is Ārya.[3]

It is clear that the peoples were divided into higher and lower ranks from the following verse of the popular Earth-hymn:

> *asaṃbādhaṃ bádhyato mánavānāṃ yasyá udvatáḥ pravatáḥ samaṃ bahu* ।
> *nānávīryā Oṣádhīryā bibhártī Pṛthıvī náḥ prathatāṃ rādhyátāṃ naḥ* ।।
>
> She, who is sufficiently wide and strong to pick up all those from higher and lower (ranks) of men and who possesses plants of various energies is the Earth and she must enrich us with food.[4]

The demarcation of the society into Brāhmaṇa, Kṣatriya and Viś is apparent as the *AV* mentions 'Brāhmaṇa' more than 50 times, 'Kṣatriya' about thirty times and 'Viś' about twenty times or so.

Parṇamaṇi-sūkta, a hymn on leaf-amulet, has the following verse, an invocation by a king when preparing to mount the divine-chair at the time of his consecration:

> *ye dhīváno Rathakārāḥ karmārā ye mánīṣiṇáḥ* ।
> *upastīnpárṇa mahyaṃ tvaṃ sarvánkṛṇvabhito janán* ।।
>
> O leaf-amulet, you must make those people present around me, who are intelligent chariot-builders and those who are very honest in their respective works.[5]

This verse indicates that there was a governing authority, such as a king, who ruled over his people, his subjects. These 'people' are termed the *Jana* in the following half of a verse:

> *Vaịvạsvạtaṃ sạṃgamánạṃ janánāṃ Yạmaṃ rājáṇaṃ*
> *hạviṣá saparyata* ı
>
> Worship with oblations the son of Vivasvāna — the king Yama — who goes with the people, i.e., the *Jana*.[6]

A very common word, *Janatā* is also used to refer to the people. The *Brahmagavi-sūkta* says:

> *ekáśatạṃ tā Jạnatạ̄ yā Bhūmịrvya'dhūnuta* ı
> *prạjáṃ hiṃsịtvā brāhmáṇīmasạṃbhạvyaṃ parábhavan* ıı
>
> Those hundred people, i.e., from *Janatā* who washed off the Earth slaying the subjects of Brāhmaṇa however went defeated and lost.[7]

The same category of people has been termed *Itarajana* at another place:

> *sodákrāmạtsetárajạnānāgácchạttāmítarajạnā upáhvayantạ*
> *tiródhạ ehīti* ı
>
> It (The great Energy) went up. It arrived at allied people, i.e., the *Itarajana*. The *Itarajana* invoked it as 'O Energy disappeared, come hither'.[8]

An *AV* verse refers to 'five states' where people who used the plough to cultivate their lands resided:

> *yasyạ̄mannáṃ Vrīhiyạvau yasyá ịmāḥ Pañcá kṛṣṭayáḥ* ı
> *Bhūmyai Pạrjanyápatnyạị namó'stu vạrṣa-médase* ıı
>
> I salute the Earth with great reverence, who is the wife of the Rain god (the Parjanya) and who fertilizes every year

and there grow Rice and Barley and thus live these people from five states cultivating (their lands).[9]

And the people in general are recognised as the common people (*samāna*) governed by a head. In the following verse, for instance, Ekavrātya expresses thus:

mūrdhā Sámānānā́ṃ bhūyāsam ।
nābhíḥ Samānānā́ṃ bhūyāsam ।।

I must be as a head of the common people and be at the centre of the common people.[10]

So it may be said of the Atharvavedic people that they did not enjoy political or religious sovereignty. They lived under the control of the governors and were engaged in agro-rural and urban works such as cultivation of land and village crafts.

Relegation of the AV

The *Atharvaveda*, in spite of being a *Veda* on the life and preoccupations of a majority of the vast population of ancient India, has been generally speaking neglected to some extent and assigned a subordinate status in the Vedic literature. In the ancient period, the *AV* was often ignored when referring to the *Veda*s though later it came to be seen as the 'Fourth *Veda*'; in the modern times, on the other hand, it is noticed that studies on the Vedic literature have focused on the *Vedatrayī*, and owing to imaginary notions and preconceptions scholars have failed to show the *AV* for what it really is, that is, predominantly a *Veda* of the masses.

A brief survey of Sanskrit literature — taken up here in three phases — with reference to the position accorded to the *AV* and the interpretation of it is necessary at this point to see how the *AV* has been generally viewed since the earliest times. This will also reveal as a corollary the significance attached to the lives and preoccupations of the common people of ancient India as the *AV* is essentially a *Veda* of the masses.

LITERATURE IN THE OLD AGE (*c.* 2500-0 BC)

The *Ṛgveda-Saṁhitā* does not mention the *AV* when stating the origin of the Vedic verses:

> *tasmā́dyaj̱ñāt sárvahuta̱ Ṛca̱ḥ Sāmā́ni jajñire* ।
>
> *Chandā́ṃsi jajñire̱ tatasmsā̱dyaju̱stasmā́dajāyata* ।।
>
> From the oblations of every kind offered in the sacrifice were produced the verses of *ṚV*, melodies of the *Sāmaveda*. The metres were borne from the same and also the verses of the *Yajurveda*.[11]

As the verses of *YV-saṁhitā* and *SV-saṁhitā* are mostly derived from the *RV-saṁhitā* for sacrificial purpose only, both of them avoid the *AV*. But it is surprising that the *AV*'s own *Śaunakīya Saṁhitā* omits the mention of this *Veda* in the verse that reads as follows:

> *Ṛcaṃ Sāma̱ yadaprā́kṣaṃ ha̱virojo̱ Ya̱ju̱rbalám* ।
>
> *e̱ṣa mā̱ tasmā̱nmā hí̱ṃsī̱dvedá pṛṣṭaḥ Śácīpate* ।।
>
> O Śacīpati (husband of Śacī) Indra, of which we interrogate you, are the *Ṛk*, *Sāma*, *Yajus* and the strength. The *Veda* may not slay me for these.[12]

The *Brāhmaṇa* texts omit the mention of *AV*, as the *Aitareya Brāhmaṇa* which while explaining the duties of the four priests of the rituals given in the *Saṁhitās* mentions three *Vedas* only:

> *yadṛcaiva Hotraṃ kriyate Yajuṣādhvaryavaṃ*
> *Sāmnodgīthaṃ . . .*
>
> As it is directed that the duty of the Hotṛ is to be performed as represented in the *ṚV*-verses, that of Adhvaryu as per *YV*-verse and of the Udgītha, i.e., Udgātṛ by *SV*-melody.[13]

The same tradition is followed by the *Brāhmaṇa* texts of the *YV* and *SV* and by the *Gopatha-Brāhmaṇa* text of the *AV*.[14]

While the *Aitareya Āraṇyaka* of the *ṚV* does not mention the name of the *AV*, the *Śāṃkhāyana Āraṇyaka* of the same *Veda* mentions *AV* for the first time. It says:

> *Oṁ Ṛcāṃ mūrdhānaṃ Yajuṣāmuttamāṅgaṃ Sāmnāṃ*
>
> *śiro'tharvaṇāṃ muṇḍamuṇḍaṃ nādhīte'dhīte vedamāhusta-*
>
> *majñaṃ śiraśchitvā'sau kurute kabandham* ।
>
> He who designates a person as a teacher of the *Veda* having not studied the heads, i.e., the meanings of the *Ṛk, Yajus, Sāman* and *AV*-verse, cuts down the head of that illiterate person, leaving him with the torso.[15]

The *AV* was later admitted in the group of the sacred texts of the Āryans but it held the fourth rank. The *AV* came to feature in the literature relating to the rituals and in relation to the cosmogonic and theosophical themes of the *Upaniṣads* which emerged in the sophisticated society of the priests and warriors. The *Vedāṅgas* also mention the *AV*, with the exceptions being the *Pāṇinīya Śikṣā, Chandaḥ-Śāstra* and the *Vedāṅga Jyotiṣa*.

LITERATURE IN THE MIDDLE AGE (*c.* AD 1-1700)

The literature comprising the religious texts was designated as the *Smārta-darśana,* which differed from the *Śrauta* literature. The *Smṛtis* of Manu, Yājñavalkya, etc., *Vālmīki-Rāmāyaṇa*, the *Mahābhārata, Purāṇas* and Ṣāyaṇa's commentaries on *Vedas* including the *AV* may feature under this head.

Manusmṛti expressly advises the priest to use the exorcism formula from the *AV* to fight the enemy.

> *śrutīratharvāṅgirasīḥ kuryādityavicārayan* ।
>
> *vākśastraṃ vai Brāhmaṇasya tena hanyādarīn dvijaḥ* ।।
>
> The Brāhmaṇa without hesitating may use the *Veda* by Aṅgiras and kill the enemy as the speech is the weapon of him (i.e., the initiated Brāhmaṇa).[16]

Yājñavalkya mentions the name of the *AV* but states that the council of the experts in the threefold knowledge can only take the action of law.[17] Śrī Rāmacandra, the hero of the *Rāmāyaṇa*, advocates the three *Vedas* to demonstrate the scholarly approach of Hanumān.[18] The *Mahābhārata* also takes notice of the *AV* as *Brahmaveda* on the one hand and praises the *Trayīvidyā* as its origin on the other.[19] Some *Purāṇas* like *Skanda*, *Viṣṇu* and *Matsya* give the name of the *AV*.[20] Sāyaṇācārya considers the knowledge of the *AV* as a root of all the branches of education and comments on this *Veda* but he still regards it as the fourth *Veda* only.[21]

All the examples related above clearly show that the *AV* was used for benefit of the priests or to reinforce the heroic supremacy of the above-mentioned two groups of the Āryans.

LITERATURE IN THE MODERN AGE (AD 1701-1990)

Sir William Jones in 1784 laid the foundation of the Royal Asiatic Society which initiated a new pattern of Sanskrit studies. The new approach highlighted the significance of the *AV-saṁhitā* as an ancient text emphasising the agro-rural and urban life of the masses of its time. Scholars from India and all around the world studied the text to know various aspects of the Vedic Indian life and went on to publish their findings.

"It reveals the religion practised by the common people with a view to achieving very many trivial objects of life as well as getting rid of multifarious real and imaginary calamities," wrote Prof. R.T.H. Griffith.[22] Prof. Maurice Bloomfield described *AV* as furnishing an almost complete picture of the ordinary life of the Vedic Hindus. Sir Benjamin Walkar admired this *Veda* as a unique text and called it an invaluable source of information regarding popular religious beliefs not modified by priestly religion. Native scholars influenced by English knowledge like Jñānakoṣakār Dr. S.V. Ketakar pointed out that the *AV* was by no means a compilation of rites applicable to ancient India as a whole. Dr. R.N. Dandekar described this *Veda* aptly as the *Veda* of the masses. Many scholars in India well-versed in English as well as in the native languages have studied the Vedic literature and have referred to the *AV* in a similar manner. Some have described it as the source of Indian folk literature while some others have agreeably focused attention on its largely neglected subject-matter. In the second and third quarters of the twentieth century, Dr. Karambelkar and Dr. N.J. Shende have published their theses on religion, culture and philosophy of *AV* which are highly valued.

It was during this modern period of Sanskrit studies that the *AV* came to be recognised as the *Veda* of the masses and introduced in Vedic studies in that sense.

Modern studies on the *AV*, however, suffer, by and large, from some serious shortcomings that cannot be overlooked. For one studies on the *AV* are very few compared to those dealing with the other Vedic texts especially the *ṚV*. Needless to say, the literature related to the *Vedatrayī* seems to have relegated writings on the *AV* to the background. In other words, the attempts of modern scholars have hardly solved the problem relating to subordination or ignoring of the *AV* among the Vedic texts. The translations, critical introductions, research articles and theses of these scholars are largely Sāyaṇa-oriented and based completely on the *Brāhmaṇa* and *Sūtra* texts of the *AV* (the *Gopatha-Brāhmaṇa*, *Vaitāna-Śrautasūtra* and *Kauśika-gṛhyasūtra,* for instance). As the supplementary texts to the *AV* are more advanced than these, there is no way that interpretations of *AV* verses made by them can be considered valid. The theme of the *Veda* is handled in the traditional manner and it covers clear-cut, broad categories, e.g., religion, culture, philosophy, medicine, magic, etc. The modern scholars have attempted to lay bare the entire society of the Atharvavedic period through their researches and not simply the life of the masses. Their works appear bookish or as documentary works owing to their ignorance of Indian agriculture and their indifference towards, and antipathy to, the common people. This lack of field experience on their part often confounds the reader — he, for instance, does not understand whether the explanation of a specific hymn quoted or referred to has any relation with the actual life of his ancestors! A few illustrations will reveal the problem. The hymns on the *Brahmaudana-sava* and the *Ajaudana-sava*[23] reflect the occasion of the farmer organising a feast on the rice farm to which his companions are invited on account of their having helped him in crop-cutting (known as 'Irjik' in Maharashtra). However, many scholars have lent the hymns a ritualistic interpretation. In another instance, the word *vahatuḥ* in the verses from the marriage-hymns has been wrongly translated as 'dowry'.[24] This word can easily means 'bride's cart' or *ḍolī* as its Sanskrit root *vaḥ* means 'to drive'.

In spite of their efforts the modern scholars have not been able to show that the *AV* is predominantly a *Veda* of the masses, i.e., a *Veda* picturing the life of the common people of the society and trying to tackle their problems. For many long centuries, thus, the *AV* has remained shrouded in darkness because of a misunderstanding of it and a general apathy towards it. However, he who is eager to know the real life-history and culture of the ancient Indian farmer and his family cannot do without re-opening the glorious pages of the *AV-saṁhitā*.

References

1. Inamgaon, Dist. Pune, Central India excavation; Excavation near Budhihaḷa, Dist. Gulbarga, North Karnataka, South India, 1989-90.
2. Please refer to Appendix 3.
3. *Atharvaveda kā subodha-bhāṣya, bhāga* 1 to 4, 4.20.8.
4. 12.1.2.
5. 3.5.6.
6. 18.1.49.
7. 5.18.12.
8. 8.10. option 5.9.
9. 12.1.42
10. 16.4.1.
11. *Ṛgveda-saṃhitā*, 10.90.9.
12. *Atharvaveda-saṃhitā Śaunakīyā*, 7.54.2.
13. *Ṛgvedīya Aitareya-Brāhmaṇa*, 5.5.33.
14. *Gopatha-Brāhmaṇa, Pūrvabhāga*, 1.6.
15. *Śāṃkhāyana Āraṇyaka*, 14.1.
16. *Manusmṛti*, 11.233.

17. *Yājñavalkyasmṛti*, 1.1.9.4.
18. *Śrīmad Vālmīki Rāmāyaṇam — Kiṣkindhākāṇḍa*, 3.28 and 29.340.
19. *Mahābhārata, Ādiparva*, 155.5, 166.6.
20. *Skanda Purāṇa, Kamalālaya Khanda, Viṣṇu Purāṇa*, 3.3.22, 3.5.14, *Matsya Purāṇa*, 215.7.
21. *Sāyaṇabhāṣyasahitā Atharvaveda-saṁhitā*, Caukhamba, *Sāyaṇa-bhāṣya-bhūmikā*, verse 8, p. 2, verse 10, p. 3.
22. *Hymns of the Atharvaveda* — Prof. R.T.H. Griffith.
23. *Atharvaveda kā subhodha-bhāṣya, bhāga* 3-9.5, p. 37, *bhāga* 4-11.1.7.
24. 14.1.8, 14.2.31.

2

Economic and Political Life

Agriculture

STRETCHING from the Himalayan foothills in the north to the southern coasts and from the east to the western hilly regions of Sahyadri, India is a land of various climes marked by one common feature — that of fertile agriculture. Surprisingly none of the ancient texts has examined the Indian agrarian system and those involved in it on such an elaborate measure or dwelt on its merits as the *AV*.

The *AV* speaks highly of the agricultural activities and the workmanship associated with them. The farmer working on the farm looks glorious and follows Viṣṇu, it says:

> *kṛṣi sáṃśito'nnátejāḥ* | *kṛṣimanu vi kráme'ḥaṃ* |
> *kṛṣyāstaṃ nirbhájāmo yo 3 smāndveṣṭi yaṃ vayaṃ dviṣmaḥ* ||

> We have directed the agriculture and brightened ourselves with the help of the food-god. Regarding the dispute relating to our farm-work with the others, I would defeat him who hates us and him whom we hate.[1]

The king Soma is praised for recognising everyone who does hard work on the farm. The agriculturist irradiates the path to heaven with the help of Soma. Shining, immortal gold grows only on the farm. The farm is like a divine cow fulfilling the desires of the farmer. The farmer is identified as an authority in the knowledge and acquirement of food:

> *yad yāmaṃ cakrurnikhananto agre kārṣivaṇā annavido na vidyayā* |
> *Vaivasvate rājani tajjuhomyatha yajñiyaṃ madhumadastu nonnam* ||

> When the son of Vivasvān (Āditya, Yama or Manu) was the king, the farmers with their knowledge, like experts in the knowledge of food, prepared a code (of agriculture) digging the soil in the beginning. I offer that (food) to the sacred fire. Our food would be as sweet as nectar.[2]

The farmer is very keen to declare himself as the great son of the Mother Earth:

> *tāsu no dhehyabhi naḥ pavasva mātā Bhūmiḥ putro ahaṃ Pṛthivyāḥ* |

> O Mother Earth take us on those (lands) of yours, I am the son of the Earth.[3]

The *AV* says that all the people must cultivate lands. Everyone must work hard and grow nutritious food. Indra, the emperor of gods, is also eager to perform his duties on the farm. The common people desire to choose their king from amongst the agriculturists. The great king Pṛthi was the first to plough the land. Work is worship. The farmer maintained his lands in such a creditable manner that his competitors in the village could not help but praise his work.[4]

LAND UNDER CULTIVATION

According to the *AV*, the soil holds the plants possessing energies of various kinds. There are rivers, oceans and large landscapes on the surface of the earth. The soil impels all of us towards progress. Our forefathers, gods, men and women of various races also resided on the land under agriculture. The soil feeds us all. The richest, irrigated farm enriches the farmer as well as his nation.

Aśvinau, it says, were the twingods who surveyed the soil. The hilly regions, the forests and farms of the states of the *AV* period are mentioned in the following verse from a beautiful earth-hymn:

> *giryáste parvátā himavanto'rányaṃ te Pṛthivi syonamástu* |
> *Babhruṃ Kṛṣṇāṃ Rohiṇīṃ Viśvarūpāṃ dhruvāṃ Bhūmiṃ Pṛthivīmindráguptāṃ* ||
> *ajīto'háto akṣato'dhyásthāṃ Pṛthivīmaham* ||

> O Earth, the hills and mountains of yours may be decorated with ice and your forests may be auspicious as ever. The lands of yours, protected by Indra and coloured pink, black, red and variously formed may be stable. Your greatness may be unconquered and be offered the sacred-food and be uninjured for ever.[5]

The soil with its attractive smell is described in one verse. It is stated that gold on the surface of the earth lies mixed with stones, rocks and the dust. The farm grows crops in all seasons. The towns develop on the surface of the earth. The soil is rich enough to produce wheat and rice. The farmer wishes to reside on such a plot which is free from pins and sticks. He should not be far away from the landscape watered by canals.[6] It appears that the Indian farmer lodged close by his farm right from the period of the *AV* in order to pay full attention to agricultural activities. It is a traditional belief in India that if a farmer resides permanently in the farmhouse, then good farmwork is possible: 'If the farmer is in the farmhouse then it is farmwork. Otherwise, there are only stones and dust' (T.N. Atre in his *Gāvagāḍā*).[7]

WATER SUPPLY

The seer Sindhudvīpa mentions various sources of water for prosperity in the following verse:

śaṃ na̱ Āpó dhanva̱nyā̱ 3: śamú santvanū̱ pyā'ḥ ।
śaṃ náḥ khani̱trimā̱ Āpa̱ḥ śamu̱ yāḥ ku̱mbha ābhṛ́tāḥ śi̱vā náḥ santu̱ varṣíkīḥ ॥

The water from deserted areas may be prosperous for us, the water supplied from the rivers may be prosperous for us all. The water obtained by digging wells and boring the mines may be prosperous for us and water stored in tanks may be prosperous for all of us. The seasonal rainwater may be prosperous for us.[8]

The *AV* mentions that motor-machines of clay-pots were assembled on the well-bores near farms to supply water to the soil under cultivation. Indian agriculture was largely dependant on the supply of rainwater but water was also dammed for use at the time of scarcity, as Sindhu-dvīpa states in a verse:

A̱po di̱vyā ácāyi̱ṣa̱ṃ rasé̱na samáprkṣmahi ।
payásvānagna̱ āgáma̱ṃ taṃ mā̱ saṃ sṛ́ja̱ varcásā ॥

We collect and store water from the sky and saturate ourselves with the water. O lightening-fire, please come to me and introduce strength within me.[9]

The sudden rainfall in the summer makes the farmer speedily collect the works on the farm — this is narrated beautifully in the *Vṛṣṭi-sūkta* by Atharvan. The rain starts suddenly with the thunderbolt and the farmers rush towards shelter. The plants grow healthy due to the medicinal properties in the rain-water. The streams of water as big as huge serpents fall on the earth. The seer says that the fire-energy named Jātavedas in the rainwater is responsible for the curative nature of the plants.[10] Dr. Dange has compared this fire-energy with the fire-deity. He has argued that in this incantation the frog-hermits have praised the lightening-fire that heated the clouds to cause rain. *Adhvaryavo-gharmiṇaḥ* is a metaphor used under theosophy in his interpretation. As far as the scientific reason of rainfall is concerned, however, it is known to be the result of a sudden fall in the density of clouds.[11]

A respected seer, Śāntāti has properly described the rain-cycle in nature. The winds drive the water-streams to fill the earth with water. The torrents of rain strengthen the crops and make them healthy. Atharvan requests the deities of 'maintenance' to open the bags of water and enrich the earth with foodgrains. This rain that comes after a long period of summer heat is stated to be very useful for cultivating the lands.

PLOUGHING OF LANDS

Viśvāmitra narrates that ploughing the lands and forming rows in the soil is the fundamental process in cultivating the farm. The farmers ride on the plough. They yoke the bulls in pairs to the wooden-yokes tied with a single rope to the plough at the end. The plough is hard like *Vajra* — the thunderbolt. The handles of the plough are expected to be stiff as they are made out of *Soma*-wood. The *kṛṣi*-deity is invoked to help them and to drive the plough easily:

> *śunaṃ súphālā vi túdantu Bhūmiṃ śunaṃ kīnāśā anú yantu vāhān* ।
> *śunāsīrā haviṣā tośámānā supippalā Oṣádhīḥ kartamas mai* ।।
>
> The sharp plough-share may furrow the soil easily. The cultivation may go smooth to the bulls (or horses). Satisfied with the oblations the ploughing may be continually fruitful up to the crop-cutting.[12]

In some regions, the plough-shares were manufactured out of the hard wood of *Khadira* and a handful of butter was repeatedly applied to them so as to make them strong and polished. After ploughing, rows were formed in the soil and crops were grown in parallel rows. This was to ensure their easy access to water, sunlight and air. The soil thus cultivated and made ready to sow the seeds was designated as *Sītā*. Oblations of clarified *Ghī*, nectar and milk were offered to the sacred fire in the *Sītā*-sacrifice to enrich the soil for better fertilization. Pandit Satavalekar interprets these oblations as the 'fertilizers'. The big sacrifices might have been performed at the start of the farm activities and the remnants in the altar such as the sacred ashes might have been utilised as 'fertilizers'.

The bulls and the bullock-carts were in use on the farms. There was no limit to the amount of hard work that *Anaḍū*, the yoked bull, could put in. This is stated by the Bhṛgus and Aṅgiras. The bullocks rubbing the soil with their legs and the farmers digging it with their arms have become something like immortal in these verses. The *AV* notes that they work hard right from their birth to the end. The horses were also yoked to help in cultivation but the bulls were mainly used for the daily laboursome work. The digging instrument was in use. It is clear from the *AV* that both manpower and animalpower were used for farmwork.[13]

THE HARVEST

The masses earned their livelihood mainly from agriculture. This *Veda* informs how the masses can be nourished by producing foodgrains and cultivation of soil. Atharvan has immensely praised rice as the greatest food-crop for people in general. Jaṭikāyana in his beautiful poetic style has described the healthy rice-crops and he, as representing the *AV-saṁhitā* or even apart from the tradition, is the first to identify the farmer as one educated in food science. In an invocation, Viśvāmitra wishes that the crops of barley grow in full strength and on an abundant scale. The *AV* shows that barley was treated as the food-god. The word *Upasadaḥ* is perhaps employed in case of the secondary crops. The remains of burnt wheat and barley have been discovered in the excavation at Mohenjo-Daro and also from excavations at Inamgaon near Pune.

The farm activities during the harvest season have been described in the *Svargaudana-sūkta*. All the members of the big joint families of farmers used to gather on the large rice farms at the time of crop-cutting. The ricegrains were made free of their stem-ends by hammering and churning the stem-branches in wooden-mortar or stone-mortar with a pestle and cleansing them in the mortar with the pestle to separate grains from the husk. Then the mixture was winnowed by using the winnowing-basket so as to make them clean. The following verse illustrates all these activities:

> *u̱lūkhále̱ musále̱ yaśca̱ carmáṇi̱ yo vā̱ śūrpé taṇḍu̱laḥ kaṇáḥ* ।
> *yaṃ vā̱ Vātó Mātạriśvā̱ pavámāno ma̱māthā̱gniṣṭaddhotā̱ suhútaṃ kṛṇotu* ।।
>
> The rice-grains, those filled-up in the mortar or those churned by the pestle or in the leather bag or winnowing basket or winnowed by the Mātariśvā wind, the Hotṛ-priest may offer to the sacred-fire as the best oblations.[14]

The blowing wind is also invoked to wash away the husk from the rice-grains. The women-peasants rinsed their palms with water so as to catch the pestle properly when cleansing the rice in the mortar. Hammering with a wooden-staff as is done to separate the dirt from the clothes, the labourers separated the husk from the rice-grains. The cleansed rice was then stored in a big soil-pot or in a vessel made of bamboo or iron. The well-constructed ditches have been referred to in the following verse:

> *u̱khā ku̱mbhī vedyā̱ṃ mā vyáthiṣṭhāḥ* ।
>
> Take care as not to destroy the mortar as well as the ditch near the altar.

Every year on the sixth new-moon day, in the month of harvest, the rice-cutting feast was arranged. The participants having drunk the *Soma*-juice had a heavy meal of rice and *Ghī* along with *Birryāṇī* and enjoyed dance with drums, flutes and the trumpet. Atharvan narrates this in a very sophisticated style in the *Virāṭa-anna-sūkta* from the *AV*. Perhaps it is this ceremony of the *AV*-time that can be traced in the Irjika of the community of agriculturists in Maharashtra state.

Abhayakāma Atharvan in one of the verses indicates the method of protecting the crops and foodgrains. Aśvinau, the twingods, are

Picture 1 : The Harvest In AV.

invoked to guard the agricultural produce from rats. The seer eagerly asks the guards to hit the rats on their heads or to put-off their teeth. The farmer lashes out at the birds especially the grasshoppers in great anguish as in the following verse:

> *Tardạ hai Pataṅgạ hai jabhyạ hā upákvasa* ।
> *Brạhmevāsáṃsthitaṃ hạvirandánta ịmān Yavạ̄nahiṃsanto apodita* ।।

> O crop-cutters, O grasshoppers go away elsewhere from hither. The oblations of the grains have not yet been offered to the Brahmā god. So, don't eat them and go elsewhere so as to leave them uninjured.[15]

Sadampuṣpā, the sunflower or Sadāphulī plant, was worshipped in order to scare away the vermins from the crops. Perhaps this plant was grown around the farm as a fencing-wall or it might have been grown as an antidote secondary crop.[16] The sand and the thorns of the Jujube plant have been found around vessels unearthed from the excavation near Inamgaon.

If classified according to the subject-matter and studied accordingly, the hymns from the *AV* eventually can be seen to emphasize

---

Description of Picture 1

śụnaṃ súfạ̄lā vi túdantụ Bhūmíṃ śụnaṃ kịnāśā anúyantu vạ̄hān, śunā sīrā hạviṣạ̄ tośámānā supippạlā Oṣádhīḥ kartamạsmai. [3.17.2]

The sharp plough-share may furrow the soil easily. The cultivation may be easy for the bulls (or horses). Satisfied by oblationary-food the ploughing may continue to the fruitful-crop-cutting.

yad yạ̄maṃ cạkrurnịkhanántọ — [6.116.1]

The workers digging the soil involve those systems in the farm-work.

ụlūkhálẹ musálẹ yaścạ . . . [10.9.26]

Those grains of rice in wooden or stone mortar have been cleansed by a pestle.

Tardạ hai Pataṅgạ hai jathyạ hā upákvasa . . . [6.50.2]

O nose-cutter, get away. O grasshopper, fly away. Get lost from here.

the agricultural process in the ancient period. One can very rightly value this text as an ancient document on Indian agriculture. It is remarkable that all these agricultural activities are carried on in the present times as well in the sequence mentioned in the *AV-saṁhitā*!

Cattle-breeding

It is sad that cattle-breeding is accorded low status today and seen as an occupation of low dignity. But in the period of the *AV*, this was not the case. Those well established in this occupation are designated Paśupatiḥ, Gopāḥ, Puṣṭapatiḥ, Paśupāla, Gopatiḥ, Gopīthaḥ and Gosakhaḥ with great respect in the *AV*-hymns. Moreover, Gosūktin and Aśvasūktin were probably names assigned to the Ātharvaṇa seers. Indra is often shown desirous of gaining cattle from the masters of the cows, his invokers. The cows and other domestic animals were counted as wealth. The people in general expected the advisory authorities to emerge from among the people involved in this occupation. Gopāḥ and Gosakhā had the educated people as their colleagues and were taught with honour:

> *śikṣeyamasmai ditseyaṃ Śacīpate manīṣiṇe* |
> *yadahaṃ Gopatiḥ syām* ||
>
> O bounteous husband of Śacī (Indra), let we literate and direct him (the shepherd) that we may also be the masters of the cows (and bullocks).[17]

The farmer of the *AV* time was fully acquainted with the knowledge of cow-breeding. He knew that if numerous cattle were in his possession, he could easily utilise them for the cultivation of land and other laboursome work to enrich the land. Usually, Indra with his wife Śacī visited the cattle-field of Kuvitsa to encourage him in his occupation.[18]

THE ANIMALS

Cattle-breeding in the *AV* time mainly involved domestic animals such as cows, bulls, horses, sheep and goats. But the *AV* also refers to wild animals such as elephants, tigers, lions, hyenas, deers and pigs and mentions camels, oxen and he-buffaloes as well. Atharvan worships the God Almighty and asks for cows, bulls and horses. He hopes that the Uṣā would enrich their homes with these animals.

The cow was accorded the most respectful place among the domestic animals. Savitṛ requests the cows and bulls to stay in his cattlefarm permanently. Brahmā welcomes the bulls and cows running towards the cattlefarm. These two kinds of animals were considered more important than the horses. It was regarded as pious to listen to the bellowing of the cows and their calves. Atharvan speaks in praise of Kāmadhenu, the divine cow, describing her beauty. The cow is called *Viśvarūpā* and *Kāmadudhā*. The names of the cows are given as Śubhrā, Kapilā and Śyāmā accordingly to their colours. The cow in the possession of a Brāhmaṇa was not meant to be slain or consumed. The Śataudanā, a kind of breed of cows, was capable of yielding milk sufficient for hundreds of people. The Vaśā cow, it appears, was qualified to be the best in all respects among the breeds of cows at the time of the *AV*. She was ready for milking at any time. Moreover, anyone — the young and the old alike — could feed her, free her for grazing and tie her to the staff in the evening. She is respected as the mother of everyone in the following verse:

> *Vaśā mātā rājanya'sya Vaśā mātā Svádhe tavá* ।
> *Vaśāyá yajña āyúdhaṃ tatáscittamájāyata* ।।
>
> Vaśā-cow is the mother of the king (or the king's vassals) and, moreover, she is motherly to you, the oblationary food. The weapon in the sacrifice as well as the mind have originated in the Vaśā-cow.[19]

The seer Kāṅkāyana says that the cow has her own calf in mind everywhere and at any time. The cow is like a treasure of money, gold, foodgrains, children and calves. Atharvan, referring to torrents of rain as milk-showers, compares all the Vedic deities with the calves. The cows are seen as having reached the highest peak of holiness.

In the hymns of the *AV*, the bullocks are honoured the most for their strength and usefulness. The bull performs the strenuous activities in numerous sacrifices. He is therefore called the master of cows, calves and of the earth as a whole. The empire of the thousands of *Gaṇadevatā* with their powers and energies occurs in every part of his body. He is like Indra among the animals. The cowpens, houses and the fencing full of strong and stout bulls and milking cows are often described in the text of the *AV*. The mighty bulls were employed for cultivation and related works. The agriculturist seems very fond of his young auburn bullcalf:

piśaṅgárūpo nabhaso váyodhā Aindraḥ śuṣmó viśvarūpo
na āgán |
āyúrasmabhyaṃ dadhát prajāṃ cá rāyaśca poṣairabhi
náḥ sacatām ||

The brown-coloured, skylike, quite young, beautiful and of various forms like those of Indra he (my young bullock) has arrived. He would achieve the long life for us and give us the children and wealth and make us strong with prosperities.[20]

The cattle-dealer, observing his young bullcalf that is strong, stout, kicking and capering about, advises the other cows to obey him in every respect.

The horses that had reached puberty were required in the horse-sacrifices and for riding. The elephants are mentioned in the *AV* as strong animals. It is hoped that all people achieve energy as that which the elephants possess.

The word *Mahiṣa* has been referred to in the *AV-saṁhitā*. The roaring he-buffalo offered delight to everyone. The god Savitṛ, it is mentioned, may gather the he-buffaloes in the sacrifice. The he-buffaloes were slain and offered as oblations in the rituals. Pandit Satavalekar has translated the word *Mahiṣa* as stronger, talking loudly but V.S. Apte has clearly stated its meaning as he-buffalo and she-buffalo. However, this animal is not seen to have formed a part of the Āryan cattlefarm initially though it had a place in Indian native settlements up to the period of the *AV*.

Kṣitipād Avi and *Pancaudana-sava* are rituals where one can come across oblations of Aja — a goat — to the sacred fire. Goats were also used to pay taxes to the king.[21]

MANAGEMENT OF CATTLE FARMS

The big cowpens were situated near farmhouses in the states such as Pañcarājyāni, Pañcamānavāḥ, Pañcajanāḥ, Vaiśāleya, Vatsa, Magadha, Vairūpa, Vairāja, Uttaraṃrāṣṭram and Gaṇa. The business of cattle-breeding was more established in these regions. The big cowpens had domestic animals of various colours but of the same breed, e.g.:

> *ye grāmyāḥ paśavó viśvarūpāḥ virūpāḥ santó bahudhai-kárūpāḥ* ।
>
> Although the animals from the villages are of various colours and wicked, they are monotonous in form.

The process of securing the cattle with a cord was in practice. Sometimes, the cowpens were situated by the side of houses in the villages. The cattle entering their shelter, kicking and capering about are beautifully depicted in the hymns of the *AV*. Brahmā invokes divinity for the cowpens to be well-provided with grass and water. The following verse notes that shelters should be built with proper care so as to maintain the sweet-milking cows in peace:

> *saṃjagmānā abibhyuṣīrasmin goṣṭhe kárīṣiṇīḥ* ।
> *bibhrátīḥ somyaṃ madhvánamīvā upetána* ॥
>
> The cattle going towards this cowpen may be fearless. The cow-dung properly drained here, the cows may live giving nectar-like sweet milk and free from every disease.[22]

Here, one may consider the word *kárīṣiṇīḥ* as formed from root, *karīṣin* and meaning cow-dung. That will lead to the meaning related to drainage-system as well as the ways to ensure better fertilization. The cattle-rearer hopes that all the animals would reside in the cowpens together and live long. The amulet made from Glomerous fig tree — the *Udumbaramaṇi* — was employed for cattlefarms of beautiful, strong cattle full of milk. The huge 'wards' held the largest of all the cattle. These wards belonged to the people collectively, right from the head of the village to the common man. The seer, in the following verse, is invoking the gods for sufficiently high and wide roofs in cattle-shelters:

> *vrajaṃ kṛṇudhvaṃ sa hi vó nṛpāṇo varmá sīvyadhvaṃ bahulā pṛthūni* |
>
> *puráḥ kṛṇudhvamāyásīradhṛṣṭā mā váḥ susroccamaso dṛṃhatātam* ||
>
> Build the wards inhabited by the herds of cows. These are our only 'drink-houses'. Centre their roofs sufficiently wide and make these lick-proof. Establish the cities of iron infrangibly. The milk-tanks of yours must be so manufactured as not to be licked at all.[23]

Kaśyapa narrates a verse concerning management of the dairyfarm:

> *śataṃ kaṃsāḥ śataṃ dogdhāráḥ śataṃ goptāro adhi pṛṣṭhe ásyāḥ* |
>
> *ye devāstasyā́ṃ prāṇanti te Vaśā́ṃ vidurekadhā* ||
>
> Hundreds of dairy-managers (or the vessels to milk in), hundreds of milkmen, hundreds of cattle riders are following the Vaśā-cow. The deities acknowledge only the Vaśā as they live because of her.[24]

V.S. Apte states that the root *kaṃs* in *kaṃsāḥ* means to command and therefore the word can be translated as the commanding authority in the dairy-farm or a dairy-manager. In the dairy-farm, along with the milkmen, the grazers, the guards and others were appointed. This proves that the business of dairy-farming was efficiently managed. The seer Uparibabhravā, for instance, states that the potent grass and tanks full of pure sweet water were placed in the cowpens:

> *prajāvátīḥ sūyaváse ruśántīḥ śuddhā Apaḥ súprapāṇe pibántīḥ* ।
>
> O cows, searching for green grass with splendid calves and drinking water from clean and pure water-supplying centres . . .

Triśoka and Priyamedhā, the Vedic seers, have referred to the meadows reserved for the grazing of the domestic animals. It was ensured that cows and other animals did not enter the grazing-fields of the enemies. The cattle-breeders were in a position to possess the hills, forests and water tanks which fed their cattle.

PRECAUTIONS IN CATTLE-BREEDING

A businessman must take good care of his business so as to achieve as much profit as he desires. In the text of the *AV*, it is likewise asserted that one must take precautions in rearing his cattle with respect to their potency, curing them of diseases and protecting them from wild animals.

The bulls, horses and he-buffaloes need to be more energetic in order to carry on the work relating to cultivation especially as reproduction results in their bodily weakness at a very important age in youth. The bulk and freshness of the goats are to be maintained as they are very much in demand for their meat. For all this, the testicles of the animals were clapped. This rite may be inferred from the hymn under the title *Klībasūkta* in the *AV-saṁhitā*.

However, the scholars object to the interpretation and employ the hymn to show that exorcism was practised by a woman to rob her unfaithful husband of his generative power. But, knowing that the Indian woman is universally acclaimed for her patience, how can one even imagine that a lady from Indian culture would be able to perform such a deed against her male partner! She will certainly advise her love, according to the *Kāntāsammita-upadeśa* — 'advice by a kind, polite wife' — or rather pout and sulk in anger or scold him at the most but, certainly, she will not even allow such an idea to enter her mind. Therefore, it seems difficult to accept Prof. R.T.H. Griffith's interpretation of this hymn as 'a woman's imprecation of her unfaithful lover'. It also seems necessary to object to the opinion of Prof. W.D. Whitney who says that it has to do with making a man impotent. Pandit S.D. Satavalekar gives a more suitable and convincing explanation: "Here in these verses the process of cutting down the sperma-genital carriers or to press down the testicles or to injure the sensation regarding intercourse of the male animals of the above-mentioned breeds, is introduced. Here the seer invoking the hymn wanted to recommend some medicinal plant also but, it is impossible to detect its name at present." However, Pandit Satavalekar does state the purpose behind this operation. Here, one may take into consideration the translation of another illustrative verse from this hymn:

> *tvaṃ vīrudhā̱ṃ śreṣṭhátamābhiśru̱tāsyóṣadhe* ।
> *i̱maṃ mé a̱dya pūrúṣaṃ klībamópa̱śínáṃ kṛdhi* ॥
>
> O plant, you who is heard to be the best among all creepers, today make my he-animal impotent, make him lie down on the bed (of grass).

The animal was tied with rope from its neck to the hind feet and was made to lie down on the bed of soft grass. But Prof. R.T.H. Griffith's translation of the same verse offers a different view: "Un-man for me today this man that, he may wear the horn of hare (or hair)." The meaning of *òpa̱śínáṃ* is not generally considered to be 'the horn of hare or hair'. Prof. Whitney has allowed this word *opas* to remain in the translation as it is but in the footnote he adds an explanation of the same as a horn-shaped ornament of the Indian lady. This kind of ornament cannot be found in any region in India. The words, *kurīra* and *kumba* are also wrongly translated as horn. Therefore, these translations as well as the interpretations of the above two authors show some amount of incorrectness.

Clapping of the testicles was done by pressing the testicles between two staffs of the *Śami*-tree. The plant used as an antiseptic was turmeric — *Haridrā*. After the operation, the turmeric powder was mixed with edible oil on the operated place. The mixture being an antiseptic was also pasted on the injured place of the animals.[25] We have discussed this point in much detail to show how the foreign scholars interpreted the rites of the *AV*-hymns wrongly due to their lack of contact with the masses and their ignorance about customs in India.

The priest Brahmā has considered the matter of healing of diseases and hygiene of the cows and other domestic animals at length. Not to be pregnant in time and the birth of a twin or a trio were seen as inauspicious omens for the entire cattle. In such a situation, the cow concerned was decattled or removed from the cowpen as she was seen as a killer of the other animals:

> *ekaikayaiṣā sṛṣṭyā saṃ bábhūva yatra gā asṛ́janta bhūtakṛtó viśvarū́pāḥ* |
> *yatrá vijāyáte yaminyápartuḥ sā paśūnkṣiṇā́ti riphatī ruśátī* ||
>
> When the cow produces one calf after another for the human being, the proper reproductive system is supposed to be in existence. But she, who gives birth to the twin or trio without the menstrual flux, seems to be a source of pain for the whole cattle.[26]

Some domestic animals made it a habit to eat non-edible substances like leather-shoe, etc. Such a type, it is advised, may be decattled for some period to allow it to overcome the bad habits or to cure it from diseases. Brahmā, the priest, was a great practitioner in such matters. Arundhati, a kind of herb, is invoked for its very powerful medicinal qualities useful in reducing the swelling of the stomach and dealing with problems relating to milk-yielding capacity:

> *A̲na̲ḍudbhya̲stvaṃ práthạmaṃ dhẹnubhya-stvamárundhati* ।
> *adhénavẹ vayásẹ śarmá yacchạ catúṣpade* ।।
>
> O the plant Arundhati, be pleasant to the yoked bulls and cows first and then also to those who have no four feet either from cows or bullocks.[27]

Atharvan recommends Jīvalā, a medicinal plant, for healing the injuries of animals caused by agricultural tools as well as weapons. He, furthermore, suggests some important measures to guard the domestic animals from wild beasts of prey such as the wolves and tigers and protect the cattle from thieves and even insects:

> *udịtastrayó akramanvyā̱ghraḥ purúṣọ vṛkáḥ* ।
> *Hiru̱gdhi yantị sindhávọ hirúgdẹvo Vana̱spatị̱rhirúnnamantu̱ śatrávaḥ* ।।
>
> Those three attacking (the cattle) vigorously — the tiger, the thief and the wolf — should flee from here. As the rivers flow down the region, these enemies should be overcome and made to kneel by this divine plant.[28]

Unfortunately not mentioned by their names, these plants are stated to be useful against the snakes also. Atharvan hopes that the three attackers mentioned in the above verse would be severely beaten up as they attack the cattle and bring ruin. It is suggested that the paths of the robbers and those of wild animals be destroyed so as to prevent the stealing of the cattle from the cattlefarms. As the robbery took place generally at night, Gopatha, a cattle-breeding seer, warns the people in this occupation to be alert at night. The guards and the watchmen may in shifts, one by one, keep watch around the cowpens, farmhouses and the cattlefields:

ye rātrímanutiṣṭhánti ye cá bhūteṣu jāgráti |
paśūnye sarvānrakṣánti te ná ātmasú jāgrati te náḥ paśuṣú jāgráti ||

Those who are employed (as guards on cattlefarm) at night and keep themselves alert among the animals, keep up all the animals consciously. Of course, they aren't watchful for themselves but for the sake of our animals.[29]

Sometimes, leopards, wolves and deceiving agile hunters used to enter the cattle-sheds silently. As the poisoners were active at night, the guards were trained to make sounds like the animals as well as to disguise themselves as scarecrows to frighten and scare away the wild animals. Uparibabhravā guides his cows in such a manner that he could keep track of the cattle on their way to the cowpens. Various kinds of malpractices where the cattle were concerned are referred to in the *AV*. The animals were stolen away and often found missing. It is said to be the work of robbers or cattle-dealers like *Paṇīs*. So, it often became necessary on the part of the cattle-breeder to take precautionary measures. Therefore, the cattle were stamped on the ears or any other part of the body. This was also done to keep an account of the animals in the cattlefarm. Viśvāmitra invokes Aśvinau thus:

lohítena svadhítinā mithunaṃ karṇáyoḥ kṛdhi |
akártāmaśvinā lakṣmā tadástu prajayá bahu ||

O Aśvinau (the twingods and physicians), mark the animals on both the ears by the hot iron-sticks so as to increase the cattle in number and for their welfare.[30]

It is seen that in the ancient times of the *AV*, the business of cattle-breeding was established both in the qualitative and quantitative sense. It flourished as if in competition with agriculture. The techniques in cattle-breeding were fairly developed. This occupation featured in the list of revenue and taxation at that time. It is indeed striking that some guidelines regarding this business provided by our ancestors are of value and in practice even today. Shri T.N. Atre notes in this respect that the British scholars expressed how the Indian farmers had established their farmhouses to the extent possible. Owing to their caste-duties and the knowledge descended through their races they, since the time of their fathers and fore-fathers, have known how to make the cattle potent and make available medicinal aids for them.[31]

Trade

It is taken for granted that the ancient Indians were dispirited to carry on trade. Some of the invasions that feature in Indian history were a result of factors relating to trade and commerce. In the middle ages, shipping and voyages were not recommended and they were seen as a sin or deeds against the religious belief. But the *AV* informs us about some facts regarding trade — indicating that the above understandings are vague — and presents some new concepts of its own.

Paṇyakāma Atharvan has addressed Indra as a trader and invoked him which makes it clear that his means of earning was the trading occupation. Commodities like milk and its various products were traded. Technical terms such as purchasing, selling, profit and loss had been established by this time, as it is seen in the following verse:

> *śunaṃ nó astu prapaṇo vikrayaścá pratipaṇaḥ phalináṃ mā kṛṇotu* |
> *idaṃ havyaṃ sáṃvidānau júṣethāṃ śunaṃ nó astu caritamutthitaṃ ca* ||

> The market must be healthy for us. The purchasing and selling may be profitable to us. Knowing this, (O Agni) receive these oblations from me kindly. Let our life be decent and progressive.[32]

Care was taken to avoid any loss in transactions. The herds of cows, bulls and horses were used as carriers of goods and were also for sale.

The merchants looked after the welfare of the customers with due politeness.

TRAVEL ROUTES AND MEANS

Devayāna-mārga and *Pitṛyāna-mārga* are referred to as open highways for trade at the time of the *AV*. *Devas* and *pitaras* were the majestic guiding authorities present on these routes. The *AV* indicates that these highways were directed towards the north. The roadlines would have been pleasant for movement in carts and on the backs of animals. Our forefathers, the seers of the Vedic period, developed these ways in a workmanlike fashion. The people went to and fro the renowned cities on these highways. Excavations at Mohenjo-Daro and Harappa have revealed signs of well-marked routes and wide roadways:

> *ye panthā́no bahavó Devayānā́ antarā Dyāvā́-Pṛthivī saṃcaránti* |
> *te mā́ juṣantāṃ payásā ghṛtena yathā́ krītvā dhanámā-harā́ṇi* ||
>
> The roadways among *Devayānas* directed towards the sky and earth may be prosperous to me with milk and *ghī* so as to grant me wealth for trade transactions.[33]

The merchant demands that all the seasons be easy for him to bear and there not be any disturbance owing to violent winds, etc.

> *nivāta id váḥ śaraṇe syā́ma* |
>
> We may lodge there in the resthouse without being disturbed by any hazardous wind.

One may note *śaraṇe* as an evidence of the resthouse on the highway. The seer of the hymns on commerce invokes the gods for good functioning of his mind and intellect. He desires that trade transactions continue smoothly and pleasantly throughout the year. Bṛhaspati may have been the guide to merchants on trade journeys.

Commandos were appointed to guard the troops of merchants. The ship is mentioned and the names of almost all big rivers flowing through the north of India have been recovered in the text of the *AV*. The word *samudra* for the sea is also mentioned here. There might have been waterways in existence and long voyages might have been arranged and undertaken as indicated by evidences from Indus civilization sites and the picture of the ship painted on a drinking vessel obtained from Inamgaon. The instrument by the name *Śakadhūma* was in use to detect the direction while travelling for trade purposes and naval purposes as part of defence. Śakadhūma, as it is defined in the *AV*, is the smoke produced from burning of a cake of cowdung. The smoke could show the direction of the wind and it was used to calculate the place to be reached on sea or in the forest. Śakadhūma is also seen exalted as the king of the constellations. Late Prof. N.J. Shende has supported this observation: "For the benefit of a person going on a journey or a merchant going out for transition, weather is predicted by means of smoke of dung (Śakadhūma)."[34]

Perhaps long ago, when the human being began thinking about give and take, the system of exchanging and thus sharing food, clothing and shelter might have come into existence and the commodities associated with these included in trading transactions. The foodgrains, animals and precious metals such as gold entered the market as wealth in general and also as the means of exchange:

stego na kṣāmatyéṣi Pṛthivīṃ Mahī no Vātá iha vántu Bhūmaú |
Mitro no atra Varúṇo yujyamáno Agnirvane na vyasṛ́ṣṭa śokám ||

As the depositor of wealth travels over the earth, the wind may blow over it. Mitra and Varuṇa may remain engaged here for us. Agni may not leave us melancholy in this forest.[35]

The milking cattle, foodgrains and gold were granted as *Dhana, Dravya* and *Vitta*, the wealth and were used generally. The Ātharvaṇa seer, Gopatha invokes ingeniously, "We should be rich in possession of the cattle and foodgrains. The deity may offer wealth to the host of the sacrifice. Don't deny the wealth of anybody and deposit it with the king. The gold is nothing but the growing rice on our farms." Indra is praised as the winner of the wealth, the Dhanañjaya. The wealth is to be utilized in the proper way, it is stated. Gopatha has mentioned goods, objects and tools as wealth. The concept of wealth was derived from the stock of commodities which were in daily use with the common people, as referred to in the *AV*.[36]

The Loan Facility

Loan facilities were provided at the time of the *AV*. The term, *Ṛṇam* was in existence. To have a loan and to return the loan with due interest was common. If the amount of loan with due interest could not be paid back to the money-lender within the given time period, it was charged as the committing of sin against the court of law. The practice of supplying foodgrains, etc. on credit and returning them back to the owner is indicated in the following verse:

> *ihaiva santaḥ prati dadma enajjīvā jīvebhyo ni harāma enat* |
> *apamityá dhānyám 1 yajjaghasāhamidaṃ tadágne anṛṇo bhávāmi* ||

> Living in this world we return the amount of loan (to the moneylender). Living, we clear the amount of others wherever they are living. The foodgrains accepted on loan are also returned and therefore, O Agni, make ourselves free of this indebtedness.[37]

Generally, the common man did not desire to have a loan. But the gambler is described as visiting many moneylenders from whom he took money as loan and finding himself hated by his creditors and his wife and mother-in-law. The gambler promised the lenders and made bets with them about the return of their money.[38]

Taxation

Those dealing with agriculture, cattle-breeding and trade had to pay some amount from their credit to the king to help him in his business of ruling the land.

> *yadrājáno vibhajánta iṣṭāpūrtasyá ṣoḍaśaṃ Yamasyāmī sábhāsadáḥ* |
>
> *avistasmātpra múñcati dattaḥ śítipātsvadhā* ||
>
> The kings, being the members of the council of Yama, enjoy one-sixth from the livestock of the subjects. So, a whitelegged (or blacklegged) goat is set free for them with the sacred food.[39]

Not any kind of tax could be levied on the Brāhmaṇas as the sacred texts strictly warned against this. The wages were estimated from the host of the rituals.

> *yatrá śulko na kriyaté abalena balíyase* |
>
> The weaker person cannot implement any tax, wage or price on the stronger one.

The revenue was related to perhaps crops, cattles and other means of living. The wine-dealers, farmers and the workers paid tax to Manu, as Jaṭikāyana has stated in his verse. The son was ready to pay the tax arrears of his father owing to a fear of committing sin against law.[40]

The Village Craftsman

As far as the *Śaunakīya Saṁhitā* of *AV* is concerned various types of crafts were practised to assist the village-communities of farmers and others.

THE ARCHITECT/HOUSEBUILDER

The *Sthapati* was one who planned and constructed the houses, shelters. He was to line out the plot and construct the walls and other parts of the building. There were tools in his hand and workers under his authority to help him in his work. The sculptor from the village community, appointed as *Sthapati*, made the bed, and constructed the arches, stone layers and bricklayers by patting and pitching (designated by the term *Sthapati* itself). The *AV-saṁhitā* praised the scholarly service of the *Sthapati* in construction of the houses and cowpens.[41]

CARPENTER, BLACKSMITH, GOLDSMITH, SCULPTOR

The *Rathakāra*, the chariot-builder in the famous verse from *AV*, 3.5.6, is certified as an intelligent sculptor and the worker of subdued mind and affections. Although the designation *Karmāra* is seen applied to all the workers of the village, the blacksmiths and goldsmiths in particular have been properly associated with it. The sculptors were respected highly in the royal court.

Tvaṣṭā was the head of the troop formed by the carpenters. He, the scholar wood-cutter, the fashioner of the building was to assemble the wooden parts and join these properly to form the roof of the shelter. The divine carpenter, *Tvaṣṭā* designed a beautiful cart for his daughter and also made a thunderbolt — *Vajra* — for Indra. The skilled blacksmiths were appointed to prepare the armours and the tools useful for various village-works. The sculptor engaged in his activity is respectfully mentioned as *Kārū*. With reference to sculptors, it is stated:

> *grāvā̱ yatra̱ vadáti Kā̱ruru̱kthaḥ 1* ।
>
> Where the churning stone (in sacrifice, as if) invokes a marvellous verse. There were expert goldsmiths to make beautiful ornaments such as Rukma from silver and gold.[42]

THE WEAVER

The process of spinning and weaving the clothes for daily use is seen implied in the *AV*. The weaver tightens the threads properly to weave them. The clothes were woven and involved the following: spinning by means of wooden pegs, arranging the fibres on a beam, attaching the beam to the loom and taking care not to cut open the threads while working on the peg. These processes lay underneath the textile-designing technique of the *AV* time:

> *ta̱ntrameké yuva̱tī Virúpe abhya̱krāmáṃ vayata̱ḥ ṣaṇmá yūkhaṃ* |
> *prānyā tantúnstiraté dha̱tte a̱nyā nāpá vṛñjāte̱ na* . . . ||
>
> Technically weaving a wear twinkling with six rays, beautiful ladies from Virāja state pass on through the sky. One from them holds the threads crosswise while another takes cares not to scatter these elsewhere.[43]

Textile and spinning, as indicated by the *AV*, was a productive business that could compete with agriculture. The art of running the fibres from the beam to the loom was highly creditable and the ladies thus used to weave the marriage-*sārī* for the bride-to-be. This indicates that the women were mainly employed in this craft. Prof. Benjamin Walkar says regarding the textile business of ancient India that, in the *Vedas*, Epics and *Purāṇas* and in the early Buddhist and Jain writings, we find many references to the textile art of India.[44]

Other Workers

The guards who worked for the owners of the houses, headquarters and wards in the villages and towns were exemplified as *Veśas*, *Pariveśas*, *Kṣattāra* and *Pariveṣṭāra*. The sentinels appointed to keep watch on the waterhouses were posted as *Kuṇḍapāyya*. There were peons to offer services at the time of sacrifices and ceremonies like the marriage-ceremony. The families of the chariot-drivers, the *Sūtas* are also referred to.

The head of the village is seen referred to in terms of *Grāmaṇī*. The troops of fishermen and watermen or sailors were named *Śamvī* and *Dhīvara* respectively. One *Tvaṣṭā* was the head of the ward of the dyers. The *Dhobī* is mentioned as *Malaga*. A class of *Viśvakarmā*s is seen referred to in many verses of this *Veda*. They might have been some keen servicemen ready to perform any work assigned to them; and so, they might have been graded as *Viśvakarmā*s. Nowadays, unfortunately, such an alert people are treated badly and hated as '*Camacā*s'. There were barbers to dress the hair and to shave. Dancers and singers to entertain the people were ready for festivals, fairs and also sacrifices of long duration.[45] Nevertheless, the families from this agro-rural region of India were divided on the basis of the works assigned to them.

The Political Institutions

Though the people from the agglomerate classes, the Viś, did not enjoy any political superiority in the ancient and medieval periods of Indian history, they were certainly involved in politics to some extent. As far as the *Śaunakīya Saṁhitā* of *AV* is concerned, one can easily make out two types of governing bodies: one of them was of the Āryan community ruling in an imperial style and another was of the common people, as Rājanya Vairāja emphasizes in the *Vrātyakāṇḍa* of the *AV*. The charms pertaining to royalty — *rājakarmāṇi* — indicate the duties and powers of the governing authorities of both the types whereas the charms to secure harmony and influence in the assembly exalt the involvement of the Viś in the political aggregations.

SABHĀ: THE ASSEMBLY

This institution consisted of brilliant politicians elected from Viś to argue on behalf of them. It was solemnly spoken of as *Nariṣṭā*, meaning favourable to Viś:

> *vi̱dma té sabhe̱ nāmá Na̱riṣṭa̱ā nāma̱ vā ási* ।
> *ye te̱ ke cá sabha̱sada̱ste mé santu̱ savắcasaḥ* ॥

> O Sabhā (the Assembly), we know your name or you are as having designation of Nariṣṭā (formed out of men) and

> those, whosoever are your members, would advocate me with due co-operation.[46]

The assembly was supposed to be mainly to assist the government to execute its plans and it acted as a legal and advisory board to the court of law.

SAMITĪ: THE LEGISLATIVE COUNCIL

This board of general councillors was elected from the Viś all over the state. It was mainly concerned with the election of a king or the Rājanya. Villages, forests, assemblies, tribes and councils were established from the Viś, as it is seen in the following verse:

> *ye grāmā̱ yadaráṇya̱ṃ yāḥ Sa̱bhā adhi̱bhūmyám* |
> *ye Sáṃgrāmāḥ Samítaya̱steṣū cārú vadema te* ||
>
> (O Earth), Whatsoever are villages, forests and whatsoever are assemblies established in this region and whatsoever are the battles fought and councils elected, we will ask for appeasement for you therein.[47]

Sometimes, the divisions formed from the Viś were to protect the masses from foreign invasions and maintain internal discipline. These troops have been designated as *Senā* in the *AV-saṁhitā*. Animal power was used along with the necessary equipments by this force that acted on behalf of the government of the *AV* time.

References

1. 10.5.34.
2. 6.116.1.
3. 12.1.12.
4. 11.1, 12.1, 6.116, 12.1, 20.65, 3.12, 8.10 option 4, 10.7, 12.5, 20.68, 8.10 option 4.
5. 12.1.11.
6. 12.1.
7. *Gāvagāḍā*, p. 196.

8. *Atharvaveda kā Subodha-bhāṣya, bhāga* 1 to 4, 1.6.4.
9. 7.89.1.
10. 1.6, 1.4, 6.69, 4.15.
11. *Saṃskṛti-sugaṃdha-Maṇḍūkabrāhamaṇa Āṇi Lokaviśvāsa*, pp. 42, 43.
12. *Atharvaveda kā Subodha-bhāṣya, bhāga* 1 to 4, 3.17.5.
13. 3.17, 10.6, 4.11, 6.92, 20.37, 65. 4.7.
14. 10.9.26.
15. 6.50.2.
16. 8.10. Option 4, 10.5, 4.34, 6.116, 142, 7.58, 12.3, 9.6. Option 1, 10.9, 13.3, 11.3.
17. 20.27.2.
18. 2.34, 16.2, 3.8, 3.10, 4.21, 12.4, 19.58, 20.22, 27, 91, 92, 19.31, 20.78.
19. 10.10.18.
20. 9, 4.22.
21. 3.22, 6.28, 19.48, 20.127, 74, 126, 3.16, 2.26, 4.21, 34, 7.75, 9.7, 5.18, 10.9, 10, 6.70, 11.1, 2.5, 9.4, 6.92, 19.25, 3.22, 5.3, 26, 20.48, 3.29, 9.5.
22. 3.14.3.
23. 19.58.4.
24. 10.10.5.
25. 6.138.
26. 3.28.1.
27. 6.59.1.
28. 4.3.1.
29. 19.48.5.
30. 6.141.2.
31. *Gāvagāḍā*, p. 129. *Atharvaveda kā Subodh-bhāṣya, bhāga* 1-4, 11.6, 3.21, 12.1, 6.75, 7.6, 8.10, 15.2, 12.3, 13.1, 12.4, 2.34, 5.22, 2.34, 3.10, 11, 13, 14, 2.26, 19.31, 59, 58, 10.10, 7.75, 20.22, 76, 4.21, 6.138, 3.28, 6.59, 4.3, 19.47-50, 7.75, 20.129, 6.141, 4.22.
32. 3.15.4.
33. 3.15.2.
34. *The Religion and Philosophy of the Atharvaveda*, p. 126.
35. *Atharvaveda kā Subodha-bhāṣya, bhāga*, 1-4, 18.1.39.
36. 18.1, 3.24, 7.18, 52, 11.1, 7.17, 19.48, 49, 20.
37. 6.117.2.
38. 6.117-119, 19.57.

39. 3.29.1.
40. 3.29, 5.19, 6.116.
41. 2.32, 5.23, 3.12, 14.
42. 9.3, 18.1, 20.35, 41, 5.12, 7.73, 20.25, 77, 9.5.
43. Vairāja — A state to the north hilly region of India.
44. *Hindu-World*, Vol. 2, p. 492.
45. 2.32, 9.6, 20.5, 12.1, 3.5, 9.2, 3.5, 10.4, 9.4, 14.2, 12.3, 12.1, 13.1, 19.17, 58, 5.19, 12.1.
46. 7.12.2.
47. 12.1.56.

3

Social Life

THE people of India, whether Āryan or non-Āryan, invoked gods in the songs of the *AV* for a permanent & comfortable shelter to live in. It is an important need of man to have a shelter or house. It requires a means of living to enrich the house. There is also the wish to decorate his home in various ways. He desires other things as well: that cooking and decorating the dishes be continually on at his home and his children, grandsons and other members of the family along with the visitors and guests enjoy a long life.

The *AV* has much information on building, decorating and prosperity of the house.

The House

The following verse is recited at the time of entering the house:

> *Iḍáyā̱ juhváto va̱yaṃ de̱vānghṛtavátā yaje* ।
> *gṛ̱hānalúbhyato va̱yaṃ saṃ viśe̱mopa̱ gomátaḥ* ।।
>
> Offering food with sacred *Ghī* we invoke the gods. Possessing homes we enter these enriched with the herds of cattle.[1]

The term *Śālā* was used with reference to the house at that time. Prof. Benjamin Walkar notes, "Śālā in the sense of house or room was frequently used in combination with other words."[2]

In the *Gṛhanirmāṇa Sūkta*, the song relating to building of the house, Brahmā invokes:

> *ihaiva dhruvāṃ ni minomi Śālāṃ* | (3.12.1)
>
> I hereby only build a steady and firm house.
>
> *dhruvā prati tiṣṭha Śāle* | (3.12.2)
>
> O house, be erect firmly.

A verse refers to its roof as follows:

> *dharuṇya'si Śāle bṛhcchándāḥ* | (3.12.3)
>
> O house, you are having fixed foundations with a big and broad roof.

The plot for the house was concrete and rigid and the roof was sufficiently high and wide. There was plenty of air, water and light surrounding it and meadows nearby were full of grass to feed the cattle. The house was by the side of the farm and was used as a farmhouse.

HOUSEBUILDING

The plot was lined out according to the plan and the required carpet area from it was selected for the construction of the building:

> *yastvā Śāle pratigṛhṇāti yena cāsi mitāṃ tvam* |
> *ubhau mānasya patni tau jīvātāṃ jaradaṣṭī* ||
>
> O residence, he who possesses you and you are measured for whom, O the Mrs. of honour, you both live long with each other till old age.[3]

It was believed that there should not be any accident in the premises of the compartment. The poles of the required height were buried in the plinth and the beams of the timber were fixed tightly with ropes on the heads of the pole. The joints were fitted in the proper way and the triangles to weigh the wooden battens were joined so as to form the slope of the roof built out of grass. The corresponding poles were joined with the mats woven out of *ratan* to form the walls and the partitions of the house and make the necessary rooms as per requirement. This is indicated in the following verse:

> *vaṃśā́nāṃ te nahánānāṃ prāṇāhasya tṛṇásya ca* |
> *pakṣā́nāṃ viśvavāre te naddhāni vi cṛ́tāmasi* ||
>
> O house, comfortable on all sides, we tie your partitions made out of grass with the mother-in-law of Garuḍa — the king of birds, the Eagle — and with the bamboos joined together.[4]

Of the materials used to build the house, one type is mentioned as *Iṭa* in the text of the *AV*. V.S. Apte translates *Iṭa* as mat, a web made of cane or grass. Another material is mentioned as *Viṭa* meaning brick in native language. The walls of the house were built of clay-bricks also in some regions. Baked clay-bricks have been found in the excavations at Mohenjo-Daro and Harappa and also at Inamgaon. Indra makes the shelters for rich owners out of three kinds of metals, as it is mentioned in the text of the *AV*. Prof. Walker writes that in architecture their style of hut has been cited as the proto-type of the barrel-haulted *caitya* (Buddhist cave temple) with its horse-shoe arch. Iron and copper smelting over surface, coal-fires was another one of their achievements which enabled them to extend their settlements through the use of metals for their weapons and fortifications.[5] Says one seer, we build as if a store high up to the sky from the earth and construct rooms as well as godowns side by side:

> *kulāye'dhí kulāyaṃ kośe kośaḥ samúbjitaḥ* |
> *tata marto vijā́yate yasmād viśvá̄ṃ prajāyáte* ||
>
> There formed a room within the room in an apartment and the underground caves one after another. And then knows the mortal being that from which the universe has originated.[6]

Dr. M.K. Davalikar states in this respect that within the colony of the sculptors and well-settled agriculturists a sufficiently big house was excavated. It was found divided into five big rooms but with an underground store in the front.[7] Separate rooms were seen for the kitchen, worship of god, dining and the ladies.

DECORATION AND PROSPERITY

At the time of the *AV* the conception of a 'graceful' house was related to the prosperity associated with it. Every one was welcomed to the house with due respect. There was not any kind of fear in the house. The houses were enriched with foodgrains. Pious, prosperous, delightful men and women were the grace and status of a house. There were a number of children along with other relations in the house. They had their meals consisting of nourished food and drinks and were stout like stones. The couple of offsprings, like the sun and the moon, would play on the ground in front of the house as it is recited in the following song:

> *pūrvā̱pa̱raṃ cárato mā̱yayai̱tau śíśū̱ krīḍánta̱u pari yāto'ṛṇa̱vam* |
> *viśvā̱nyo bhuvánā vi̱caṣṭá ṛtūnra̱nyo vi̱dadhánjāyase̱ naváḥ* ||
>
> The two children together rejoicing in a magical-play, set beyond the sea one after the other. One out of them holds the universe as a whole whereas the other possessing seasons rises anew every night.[8]

The wife and the husband were regarded as the focus of charm in the residence. The arrival of an *atithi* — a person paying a surprise-visit — was accorded religious status. The healthiness of the body and mind, friendliness among the members and very high regard for visitors were important merits for the decoration of the house rather than external beauty as seen in tiles and colours, etc.[9]

Food and Drinks

The kitchen, situated separately in the house, was the *Pāka-śālā*. A sufficient amount of food was prepared on occasions like sacrifices, marriages, etc. The men went into the forests to search for

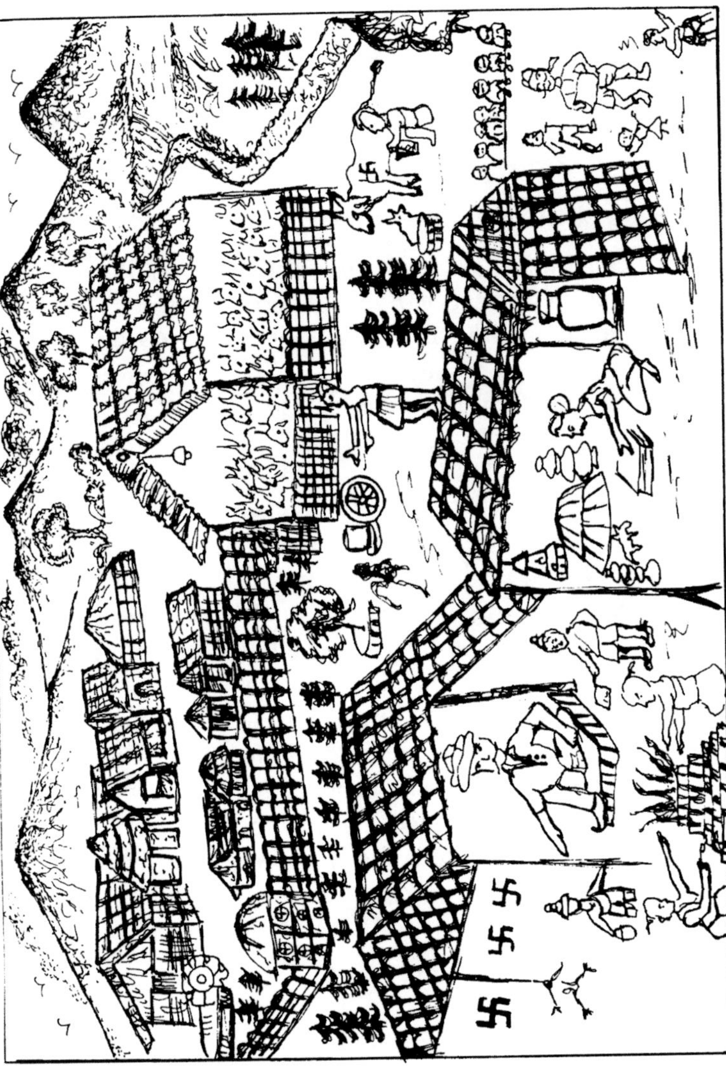

Picture 2 : The Standard of Living and the Literature of the Masses. House-building:

Vaṃśā́nāṃ te nahánānāṃ . . . 9.3.4. O House comfortable, . . . with your bamboos joined together.

groundnuts, sweet-roots and hunt for meat. They were also in charge of the heavy work on the farm and guarding the herds of cattle. On the other hand, the ladies had to milk the cows, pound the foodgrains and cook the food.

The food was prepared out of rice, barley and wheat by forming cakes that were *capātī*-like. *Ghī* and butter were preferred. To prepare the food, to cook are referred to in holy terms in the *AV*:

> *eṣa yajñānāṃ vitáto bahiṣ́ṭho viṣṭāriṇáṃ paktvā divamāviveśa* I . . .
> *upá tvā tiṣṭhantu puṣkariṇīḥ samántāḥ* II
>
> This (sacrifice), the largest and the outmost of all the sacrifices, sitting on the seats of *Kuśa*s (a holy-grass spread to prepare seats around the altar in sacrifice) and cooking the offerings, climbed on to the heaven. . . . The tank full of lotus might be ready for you around.[10]

The lunch was made out of lotus-nuts, musculous roots, milk and honey. The milk and milk-products have been repeatedly praised as proteinous food. Cooking with rice and meat is variably described in the *Brahmaudanasava* and the *Ajaudanasava*. The *Soma* was preferred as a drink and it was everybody's favourite at the time of this *Veda* also. *Surā-madya,* the liquor, was offered as a drink to those who accomplished meritorious deeds, which were especially performed by warriors.[11] But, Prof. Benjamin Walkar notes the lower status associated with the drink. In the *Atharvaveda, Surā* is referred to as the reward for the performance of duty but in general it had an evil reputation and was condemned by the law-givers as a cause of wrongdoing, giving rise to broils in assemblies.[12]

Clothes, Hair-style and Make-up, Ornaments

Regarding dressing or wearing clothes, an *AV* verse states:

> *pari dhatta dhatta no varcásemam . . . Bṛhaspatiḥ prāyácchadvāsá etat* II

> Put on this cloth. O, put-on for your lustrous appearance . . . The Bṛhaspati has offered this wearings for you to achieve prosperity.[13]

Rohita, a shining sun puts on his divine overcoat. A precious garment worn as 'overcloth' is seen specially designed for ladies under the name *Drāpī*.

> *ya ime Dyāvāpṛthivī jajāna yo drāpiṃ kṛtvā bhuvanāni vaste* || (13.3.1)

The inners are also mentioned in the marriage-hymn:

> *yadā sandyāmupadhāne yad vopavāsane kṛtam* || (14.2.65.)

The blanket was used to protect the body from the cold.

The fifteenth book of the *AV* has also referred to Ekavrātya's clothes, hairstyle, hat, ornaments and other items of decoration. The common *Vrātya* wore a piece of cloth on the lower part of the body and another on top with a head-dress of a particular fashion of *Feṭā* or *Paṭakā* which was not very different from the head-dress of the farmer of the fifties in the regions of India. The ladies wore *Sārī*s folded in the front as per the description of the well-dressed bride in the *Vivāhasūkta*. Women covered their breasts. Some prayers reflect a wish for soft and smooth clothes, delightful to touch:

> *yat te vāsaḥ paridhānaṃ yāṃ nīviṃ kṛṇuṣe tvam* |
> *śivaṃ te tanve 3 tat kṛṇmaḥ saṃsparśedrūkṣṇam-astu te* ||
>
> The wearing that you have, of which you have arranged the foldings, is well-wishing you and seems very smooth to touch.[14]

It was a fashion to dress and set the hair in a proper style at the time of the *AV*. Hair-cutting as well as shaving the beard were in practice, as the references in the marriage hymns show. The hair of the bridegroom was cut and his beard was shaved off with a blade by the barber.

To decorate eyes with *Kajjala*, to make up the face with talc powder and creams and to put on one or two ornaments was considered as high prestige:

> *yaḥ āktākṣáḥ subhyaktaḥ sumáṇiḥ suhíraṇyaváḥ* ।
> *subráhmā Brahmáṇaḥ putrastotā kalpéṣu saṃmitá* ।।
>
> A good son of Brāhmaṇa, the Brahmā-priest, who applies *Añjana* in eyes, uses creams, puts on jewels and golden ornaments is granted as scholar reciter of the praising hymns up to the end of millions of years — the *Kalpās*.[15]

There were precious jewels in the market and items like a shining golden necklace — a *Niṣka* — was wished for in dreams. Recites a seer thus in one of the verses:

> *anāsmākastaddévapīyuḥ piyárurniṣkamiva pratímuñcatām* ।
> *navároatnīnapámayā asmākaṃ tataḥ parí* । *duṣvapnyaṃ sarváṃ dviṣate nirdáyāmasi* ।।
>
> A person, a worshipper of god and not of ours and who has a body-colour as of golden *Niṣka*, let leave him. Stealing the new jewels around from us, O you bad dream, be troublesome to our enemy.[16]

The ornaments prepared of gold, silver and copper with coloured stones within, the crown made of gold, silver and designed somewhat like a fan, ear-rings, rings, belts, bracelets, collyrium powder, colours, nail-paints and body-paints, and green clay-stones have been derived from the excavations.[17]

Fairs and Festivals

The people assembled to enjoy the eating and drinking. Variety entertainment was arranged and it featured silly questions, proverbs, jokes and jests as is described in the *Kuntāpa* hymns. Gambling was played as a favourite game at the time of the *AV*. Fairs were arranged and festivals were celebrated. *Indramahotsava, Gomahotsava* and *Navānnamohotsava* were the events to be enjoyed. On occasions of marriage, fairs and festivals, the people dressed well and decorated themselves to sing and dance to the accompaniment of drums and enjoyed the ceremony.[18]

Bad Habits and Practices

The people in general possessed some bad habits and committed offences. The people of *AV* time were certainly not an exception to such characteristics as part of the personality. The hostile magical part of this *Veda*, if seen from this particular viewpoint, indicates some vicious practices of the common people at that time and also some offences committed by them.

GAMBLING

It involved the use of dice on two platforms of clothes arranged to make a cross and painted with squares. Gambling was a common game of great interest all over that entertained the people. Gambling involved politics and decided war affairs. There were big porches for dice-throwing as is mentioned in the *AV*. The platform was created specially for the purpose, a chequered board or a cloth was arranged properly and throwing dice on the *paṭa*, the game was played to achieve fruits merited as *kṛta, tretā, dvāpara* and *kali*. This game is commented upon in detail under the title *Akṣasūkta* in the *ṚV*. This autobiography of a person addicted to gambling is beautiful poetry. The gambling, at a later stage, became a bad habit because of the disadvantages it resulted in. As understood at the time of the *AV* the *Apsarās* — the nymphs — held everyone in expectation in dice-playing. These courtesans of gods offered fruits to the participants depending upon the results of the game. As the thunderbolt dashes down a tree violently, so the game of dice thrusts down a person addicted to it:

yathā́ vṛkṣamaśanirviśvā́hā hantyáprati |
evā́hamadya kitavā́nakṣairbádhyāsamaprati ||

As an ever destroying thunderbolt surely kills a tree on dashing it down, I would tie the gambler with dice to ruin today.[19]

A gambler, apologising, bows down before the dice. Once in the court of dice, he says, he feels no sense of the body or the mind. Sometimes he utters restlessly due to his defeat in a game as the dice may be mingled with the dust and sand that is to be utterly destroyed. The Apsarāḥ, the goddess of dice, looks fiercely at the gambler who has achieved total failure in the game. The lady moneylender talks badly of him and sends him away from her house. The gambler becomes wicked at the end. To come in the grasp of the dice was understood as succumbing to a vicious practice at the time of the *AV*. For the gambler within the compass of the dice goes completely mad. He very often wickedly invokes the dice as seen in the following verse:

idamugrāyá babhrave namo yo akṣeṣú tanūvaśī |
ghṛtena kalíṃ śikṣāmi sa nó mṛdātīdṛśé ||

I pay reverence to the fierce, pink-coloured dice overpowering my body on every side. Offering the sacrificial *Ghī* to the kali result, I request it to forgive me on its way.[20]

The gambler felt himself bound by the spirit of emulation towards his rivals to win the game. However, he even dared to supplicate the dice to kill his competitor as it is seen in the following verse:

sapatnáṃ me kitavaṃ rándhayantu |
vṛkṣamivā́śanyá jahi yo'smānprátidīvyáti ||

As a thunderbolt draggling along, rolling about, burns the tree, O dice, oppress and rub the rival player of mine to die soon.[21]

USE OF ABUSIVE LANGUAGE

Talking in vain or using wild, threatening language was highly prevalent at the time of the *AV*. A person talking in this fashion has been blamed as a defaulter in one of the verses:

> *Indrásya ma̱nyavé jā̱lmā ā vṛ́ścante̱ acíttyā* । (12.4.51)
>
> Owing to the anger of Indra, the people using unbridled speech are to be slain.

ADULTERY

Although the custom of polygamy was in existence, the men proclaimed their vigorous passionate desire for women in many mischievous ways as is indicated by the hymns of the *AV*. This was rather a problem giving rise to many others such as jealousy towards the rival women, use of wild, magical spells against men and women and blind faiths of various kinds in the society in general.[22]

MISERLINESS

Miserliness is mentioned as 'Ākūti' and the people are warned of it. The goddess Ākūti, it is said, takes away one's clothes and torments him badly. Miserliness often misguides the common people mischievously and forces them to behave as disagreeable persons:

> *u̱ta na̱gnā bobhúvatī svapna̱yā sácase̱ janám* ।
> *aráte ci̱ttaṃ vīrtsa̱ntyākū́ti̱ṃ purú̱ṣasya ca* ॥
>
> O the devilish Ākūti, the naked you dreaming badly disturbs the people violently and moreover torments their hearts to behave like wicked persons.[23]

At the time of war, to confuse or rather hypnotize the enemy warriors by intoxicating them, some frolics have been stated in the text of the *AV*. But unfortunately later on these resulted in addiction in the life of the common man.[24]

Violence in Society

We observe much flexibility in the social life of the people of the Vedic times. The masses had to face war every now and then and so were often confronted by critical situations. The conquerors used to treat the defeated persons very severely. Moreover, the masses had to face violence from the invaders without any crime on their part. The battlefield and the state under war were reduced to dust and the defeated subjects were made slaves — the *Dāsas* who had to do laboursome work for the winners. The terrorists practised violence against the commons. The common people employed benedictions through spells to overcome the violence (killing and beating) inflicted and vigorously rebuked the invaders in their invocations:

> *dauṣvápnyaṃ daurjívityaṃ rakṣó abhva'marāyya':* |
> *durṇāmnīḥ sarvā́ durvācastā asmannā́śayāmasi* ||
>
> O the goddess of war, the defaulters acquiring our livestock violently, the demons wanting us to die immediately and using abusive language towards us, O evil naming one, would be taken away so as not to stay with us.[25]

THEFT OR ROBBERY

The robbers called *Attrin, Viṣkandha, Taskara* and *Stena* stole the cattle. They often destroyed the crops full of foodgrains and tormented the women and children. They arranged the thieving and pilfering activities usually in the dark 'no-moon' nights and took away all the livestock from the household and the farmhouse. The robbers who stole from the travellers on roads are designated as *Viṣkandha*. They wildly slew the cows and other domestic animals and even the men and women as it is described in the lead-amulet hymn:

> *yadí no gāṃ haṃsi yadyaśvaṃ yadi pūrúṣam* |
> *taṃ tvā Sīséna vidhyāmo yathā no'so avírahā* ||
>
> O Viṣkandha, slaying our cows, horses and the brave man,

> we would hurt you with the lead-amulet and prevent you from slaying our warriors.[26]

Not everyone met with the *Piśāccas* — the goblins, the thieves and the people wandering in the forests — because, they were seen hanging over the animals and also human beings from civil lanes tied by ropes around their necks.

SLAUGHTER AND RAVAGE

The Dasyūs and Kimīdinas were found beating others so as to slaughter and ravage the people. These people laid hold of anybody and behaved wildly like animals.

> *kimīdine kimidānīmiti carate kimidaṃ kimidamiti vā piśunāya carate* | *(Nighaṇṭu*, 4.3, *Nirukta,* 6.11)
>
> Kimīdinas attack the defaulters, achieving their livelihood by wandering with questions such as what or what it is and also behave like wild animals.

They used to employ magical spells against the common people and acting as relatives — for example, as father and mother — introduced themselves in the civil lanes to take advantage of the ignorant and those given to blind faiths. The deceiving Arjunīs and the liar Bharujīs with a pleasing — and sometimes also with flattering — dialect behaved mischievously with the common man.

THREATENING, TERRORISM, KIDNAPPING

There were people with the habit of threatening others, snubbing others and displaying a voilent temperament at all times. They behaved like demons with the common people, especially with the women, to drive them out of their households. They were called *Sadānvā*:

> *niḥ sālāṃ dhṛṣṇuṃ dhiṣaṇámekavādyāṃ jíghatsva'm* |
> *sarvāścaṇḍásya naptyo'nāśayámaḥ Sadānváḥ* ||

> We slay down the Sadānvās who drive out one from the household, threaten others, quarrel with and use abusive words against each other, kill anybody and are grandsons of the people indulging in terror over all.[27]

These people termed as *Sadānvās* stole sheeps and goats from the herds of cattle and also girls and women from their wards. They created a lot of trouble in the society. Although they lodged within buildings, lived in the society along with their families and acted with familiarity towards all, they committed offences against the common people. The text of the *AV* says that they should be ruined at the earliest.

POISONING

Poison was used to destroy the competitor in business, the rival in gambling and the rival wives and their sons.

> *vāridaṃ vārayātai varaṇāvátyāmadhi* |
> *tatrāmṛtasyāsiktaṃ tenā te vāraye viṣam* ||
>
> A man giving poison would be defeated from Varaṇāvati and sprinkling the *Amṛta* — a drink worshipped for immortality — there I would prevent your poisoning.[28]

Magical spells were employed by a woman to eradicate the rival-wife, to bring her own husband to subjection and to get herself satisfied even in the physical and mental condition imposed on her by wizards. Rites were performed to practise crimes such as paralysing others, bewildering others, begetting hatred, eradicating a person, seduction and slaying persons.[29] Magical spells were used to scare away the enemy.

PUNISHMENT

At the time of the *AV* the offenders were charged and punished.

Agni and Indra, it is mentioned, would take the Yātudhāna, Kimīdina, Dasyū and Attrina in possession and punish them. They would be captured and beaten till death. The Yātudhānas, moreover, should be beaten and made to cry. The offenders of all types would be thrusted up by Agni in such a way that they would themselves bend down and hand over themselves to the prosecution. But the idea of *Prāyaścittam* is not sufficiently clear as we cannot understand whether the man charged with the crime could get excused from the punishment after going through expiation or not. The magicians were hung by rope and killed thereafter. The amulet of lead — the *Sisamaṇī* — has seen instrumented in magical charms against such offenders. The Yātudhānas and Kimīdinas were burnt immediately. The Yātudhānī was so harassed that going mad she would start blaming herself:

> *putramáttu Yātudhā̱nīḥ svasā́ramu̱ta na̱ptyám* |
> *adhā́ mi̱tho vike̱śyo̱ 3 vi ghnátā̱m Yātudhā̱nyo̱ 3 vitṛ́h yantāmarā̱yyáḥ* ||
>
> The Yāthudhānī would slay her own son and daughter and also her grandson to arrange her own meal and with scattering hair she would start beating everyone from her own family.[30]

The Śerabha, Śerabhaka, Kimīdinas, Śevṛdhaka, Śevṛdha, Mroka, Anumroka, Upabdi, Arujunī and Bharujī were made to eat their own flesh as punishment. The Dasyūs were pierced with arrows till death. The seer named Cātana oppressed the offenders so severely that the *Piśāccas*, *Stenas* and *Vanecaras* ran away on hearing the name of this seer. As dogs in front of the lion and mosquitoes at the feet of an elephant, the dubious offenders lay down in weakness on the steps in the court of Cātana.

The reproductive organ of a man behaving violently with a women was pricked with a sharp needle. The Mūradeos had their legs cut and their skins removed and were burnt to ashes for their crimes against polite people. The offenders were broken in the ribs and had their foot cut off. Magicians were imprisoned and made to lie-down on ice-beds. Their necks were also cut away. The evil practitioners were not allowed to enter the civil lanes and were beaten with stones if they entered. They were driven out of their native places immediately.

The common people took precautions to ensure that they did not commit any transgression as they feared the strict laws and regulations executed by the home department of the *AV* time. A person slew himself rather than be charged with criminal offence and called a thief, robber, magician or terrorist:[31]

> *yadí Yātudhāno'smi yadi vā pūrúṣasya āyúḥ tatapa adyā múrīya* | 8.4.15.

Religion and Worship

It is indeed irksome when one is asked to consider whether a conception like religion existed in the life of the common people in the Vedic times. The *AV-saṁhitā* corrupted by the rest of the Vedic literature interprets two streams of notions about '*Dharmāṇi*' — the religion. The Āryan priestly religion as revealed in this text has, to a large extent, descended from the *ṚV*. But here, Vedic deities such as Agni and Indra have become idols in the hands of priests instead of inspiring the Vedic seers by their noble nature as seen in the *ṚV*. They are invoked and lauded in matters such as killing of demons, overpowering the magician-men, introducing magical powers for curing diseases and for overall prosperity to kings and warriors. The ritualistic deeds were started among the people in common to achieve better cultivation in the lands under agriculture, prosperity in trade and commerce and success in every kind of work, whether requiring manual labour or intellectual. There was another class of magician-men who employed sorcery through spell and invoked verses through exorcism on behalf of a person possessed by demons, goblins, demigods and nymphs. These priests performed magical practices of various kinds for the masses. The common people in general, in spite of their laboursome, hard and productive work, came under the impact of the religion and worship that originated in Vedic mythology and involved mysticism through magic — holy or hostile.

Folk Literature and Songs

Mahamahopadhyaya Citrav Shastri terms the Atharvavedic poetry as the pious origin Gaṅgotrī — the origin of Gaṅgeśa — of the folklores perserved by the common people of India.[32] The *AV* as a source of folk literature and as a study of Indian poetics greatly stimulated the minds of foreign scholars in the eighteenth century. Modern critics in native languages have critically edited many folk songs, especially women scholars like Durga Bhagwat, Dr. Sarojini Babar in Marathi, from the topographical region of Maharashtra. They have very enthusiastically pointed out that these songs are not attributed to a particular author and these have originated among the common village people occupied in their daily tasks such as agriculture. A student of the *AV* may study the *AV* songs to find some points of agreement between them and the songs of the village folk at least in respect of the theme and the poetic style. For example, the *AV* farmer started his work of cultivating the land, singing:

> *yunakta sīrā vi yugā tánota kṛte yonaú vapate ha bījám* ।

and he paid reverence to the goddess of agriculture with

> *Sīte vandā́mahe tvārvā́cī subhage bhava* ।
>
> Yoke the plough, yoke the pair of bulls and having designed the soil in rows, sow the seeds. O the goddess of field, we bow down before you for you to be prosperous in your speech.[33]

The Marāṭhī farmer also sings at the time of cultivation:

> *nāṅgarāna nāṅgarala vakharāna vakharala*
> *tifanībāile siṅgāruna setī nela*
> *ārati ovāḷū tifanī . . .*
>
> The land under agriculture is yoked by the plough, weeded and cleaned by scuffler and decorated sowing-harrow is brought to the farm. O, we worship the sowing-harrow with holy-candle.[34]

The point of similarity is clear between the two songs relating to shooing away of birds spoiling the corns. The *AV* farmer said:

> *Tardạ hai Pataṅgạ hai jabhyạ hā upákvasa* |
>
> O nose-cutters, get away. O grasshoppers, fly away.[35]

In the same way, the farmer at present sings:

> *āra āra pākhrā yevū nạka yevū naka an ḍoḷā pikāvara ṭhevụ naka* ||
>
> O ye bird, don't come here and don't even look at our crops.[36]

The women in India, perhaps illiterate, have traditionally originated interesting lores from imagination of day-to-day life including domestic matters such as enmity with the rival wife. In the following song, a lady imposes her right of advocating in the household:

> *ạhaṃ vádāmị nettvaṃ sạbhāyạ̄mahạ tvaṃ vadá* |
> *mamedasạstvaṃ keválọ nānyāsā́ṃ kị́rtayā́ścạna* ||
>
> O my dear Mr., you may deliver your speech out in the assembly but, I am here to enunciate my opinion in my house and you must be mine only. Don't even mention the name of any rival wife.[37]

And the goddess of the Marāṭhī lady, Rukmiṇī rebukes her husband Viṭhṭhala somewhat lovingly:

> *Rukmīṇa bola "Mājhyā Viṭhṭhalā pirtīcyā* |
> *vāḍyālā nakā jāū tuḷaśī garatīcyā* ||
>
> Rukmiṇī, the goddess-wife of Viṭhṭhala, says, "O my love Viṭhṭhala, don't go out for the palace of amorous Tuḷaśī."[38]

In marriage ceremonies along with dances, the two sides would tease each other as, for example, the bridegroom by ladies of the bride party through the middleman. In the following verse, the middleman is a barber:

> *yat kṣuren̥á marcayátā sutejasā vaptā vapási keśaśmaśru* |
> *śubhaṃ mukhaṃ mā na āyuḥ pra móṣīḥ* ||
>
> O barber brother, as you are to dress the hair and to shave the beard of our brother-in-law with a sharp lustrous knife, please polish his face with your soft palms so as to make it shine with reverence and be aware that his life must not be cut down.[39]

In Marāṭhī marriages a similar song is sung:

> *sonyācā vastarā nhāvīdādā tu caturā, haḷūñca cucakārā* |
> *Laxmī āī dharī ghaḍī* | *Telaṇīcī viḍī* ||
>
> O bounteous barber-brother with golden knife, be aware and polish smoothly the face of our bridegroom. During his bath, the mothergoddess Lakṣmī holds the towel for him, and what nonsense of the lady oil-merchant is this that she is enjoying her smoking with *viḍī* here in this marriage *paṇḍāl.*[40]

A number of assertions by oaths, proverbs and silly questions from Kuntāpa-hymns of the *AV* are similar to such types of Marāṭhī songs.[41] Teasing and taunting the girls who were especially young and pubert on occasions like marriage and the midday period of the ritual, etc., have been represented in a highly satirical style as in the following verse:

> *yaṃ kúmārī piṅgalikā kṛśitaṃ pīvárī labhét* |
> *tailakuṇḍā diváṅguṣṭham radántaṃ śuddhamuddháret* ||
>
> O, if this fat miss were to meet in marriage with any poor creature, a weak young boy, she would certainly oppress him like a vessel full of oil oppresses the thumb holding it.

A Marāṭhī mother bursts out at her daughter who has the habit of wandering from house to house in the village and to her son who does the same:

> *leka mājhī havaī nī gharogharī jāvaī,*
>
> *lyoka mājhā dānā nī gharoghara sunā* ।
>
> O, my daughter is like a nightingale possessing my sons-in-law everywhere in our village and my dear son is like that too, giving kindly everything in his possession to every girl so that I have daughters-in-law everywhere in my village.[42]

It would be appropriate to close this topic with the mention of some *AV* songs sung to achieve prosperity in crops and the herds of cattle, etc. which seem identical to those designated as 'Ude-geeta' in the Goṃdhaḷī cult of the Mahārāṣṭrian villages. The *AV* verse runs as follows:

> *udénaṃ bhagó agrabhīdudénaṃ Somó Aṃśumān,*
>
> *udénaṃ Maruto devā udindrāgnī svastaye* ।
>
> *udyate namá udāyate nama uditāya namáḥ,*
>
> *udihi udihi Sūrya varcásāmābhyudihi* ॥
>
> The god of prosperity would arise for him. Aṃśumāna — the lustrous one Soma would arise soon for him. The gods Maruts, Indra and Agni would approach him soon for better prospects. We address them, render obeisance and worship with oblations and salutations the deities rising up. O sungod, please arise, arise with your lustrous light.[43]

The Marāṭhī song has the following to say:

> *Aṃbābāīcā udo udo Māhuranagaḍa Reṇuke goṃdhaḷā ye.*
>
> *Tuḷajāpūr Bhavānī goṃdhaḷā ye.*
>
> *māyecā nijarūpa āīcā goṃdhaḷā māṃḍīlā . . .*
>
> *ude ude ga Aṃbābāī goṃdhaḷā ye.*
>
> *namana ho namana, namana namana, Bhairubā devālā gā*

Picture 3 : The Standard of Living and the Literature of the Masses. Marāṭhī song belonging to the Goṃdhaḷī cult—
Aṃbābāīca udo udo . . . māyecā nijarūpa āīcā goṃdhaḷa māṇḍilā . . . ude ude ga Aṃbābāī . . . goṃdhaḷā ye.

Mayāppā rājālā . . .
Gaṇūbā devālā gā piratīmipāḷālā, namana ho namana,
namana ho namana. . .

We respect our mother goddess Aṃbābāī saying *ude, ude,* i.e., O arise, O arise. We have arranged a worshipping rite *goṃdhaḷa* for our mother goddess Ambābāī. O Reṇukā, from Māhurana fort come to receive our worshipping rite. O Bhavānī, from Tuḷajāpūr, come to have our worshipping rite. O Ambābāī, O arise, arise O, and please come to receive the oblations in our worshipping rite *goṃdhaḷa*. We salute again and again the god Bhairubā, the king of our gods, Mayāppā and we salute repeatedly god Gaṇūbā who looks after the whole Earth and we salute again and again.[44]

The neglect of the *AV* by the traditional literature is an indication of the verses of *AV* being the literature of the downtroddens or Dalit literature of that time. Moreover, an astonishing feature of these *AV* songs is realised — that is, the ancient Indian Vedic origin of the folk literature along with the Dalit literature edited in native Indian languages of the present time.

Interaction between Various Groups

Up to the *AV* period, the Āryans along with their 'Viś' — community in general — resided in the northern region of India whereas the non-Āryans were settled independently in the same region as well as in parts of southern India. The Indian Āryans became a food-producing people from a food-gathering people. The natives were established according to their standard of living in villages as well as urban areas.

The Āryans often came in contact with many native tribes including that of the Vrātyas. Actually, the Āryans after their invasion or migration — whatever it may have been — to India, assimilated themselves into the native groups up to some extent and non-fighting classes developed out of them as Viś. There existed a parallel group of natives who were beyond Āryan invasion; they were situated by the sites of the Āryan states and in the remaining areas of India. Those non-Āryans, preserving their own customs, have been termed the Vrātyas in the literature of the Vedic Āryans.

THE VRĀTYAS

Vājasaneyi-saṁhitā, for instance, mentions the Vrātyas in oblations offered to the demi-gods and nymphs: *Gandharvāpsarobhyovrātyam* (30.8), whereas Sāyaṇa criticizes this cult of people as those beyond the Āryan faculty of impressions: *Vrātyaṃ śāstrīya saṃskārahīnaṃ puruṣaṃ*. Where the modernists — the Westerners — are concerned, they also interpret Vrātyas as somewhat stragglers and obnoxious. However, *Śaunakīya-saṃhitā* of *AV* views the Vrātyas in its fifteenth book with sentimentality. The Vrātya cult with their leader Ekavrātya, it is said, arrived there and initiated Prajāpati, the god of creation. These people had bellies of blue and red colours. Along with their leaders, they created all the regions towards the east and the southern regions. They appointed Rājanya Ekavrātya as their leader who ruled over his lands with a benign policy towards his subjects (*AV*, 15.1-3). Among his officials were the Bhava, Śarva and Īśāna. The *AV-saṁhitā* narrates that Yati, Vala, Brāhmaṇas from the non-Āryans were the constituents of the native Vrātas. A verse on the healing property of the syrup from Daśavṛkṣa tree refers to Vrāta:

> *āgādudágādayaṃ jīvānāṃ vrātamapyágāt* ।
> *abhūdu putrāṇáṃ pitā nṛṇāṃ ca bhagávattamaḥ* ।।
>
> O he (the patient), came in full conscious, stood up and also went to his Vrāta, alive. How splendid! he as a father achieved his son and all virtue in his kinsmen.[45]

THE PAṆĪS

Indian trade and commerce is seen mirrored in the *AV-saṁhitā* in the background of the polite behaviour of merchants in general. But trading is totally related to money matters and so, corruption is hard to rule out. Some kinds of corruptions were in practice at the time of the *AV* also. The Paṇīs, a trading community of the Vedic age, were blamed for mischievous practices in transactions as well as for some bad omens. The *AV* has many references to the Paṇīs. It says that the Paṇīs should be put below dignity and they should be crawling owing to their mischievous nature. Atharvan invokes Varuṇa in a verse stating that it would be better if the Paṇīs did not know about the bad achievements:

> *tvaṃ hyá 1 ṅga Váruṇa bravīṣi punármaghesvavadyāni bhūri* |
> *mo ṣu Paṇiṁ rabhye 3 tāváto bhūnmā tvá vocannarādhasaṃ janásaḥ* ||

> O fatherly Varuṇa, there happened many mischiefs regarding the wealth as you have been charged. Paṇīs should not come to know of these and you might not be called poor.[46]

The *AV* notes that the bounteous warrior, Indra seized the Paṇīs' cows and they began to cry. The emperor is asked to thrust a blow at the Paṇīs, as expressed in the text. On one hand, the mischievousness, thievishness and corrupt nature of the Paṇīs is seen exaggeratedly narrated and on the other hand, Gautama, a Vedic seer, advises his cattle to have benedictions from them. The Paṇīs, it is said, neither themselves achieve any surplus from the wealth nor prepare it for the enjoyment of the gods. The Paṇīs of such a kind should be driven out from the well-settled community, says the *AV-saṁhitā*. The Paṇīs willing to improve themselves may, however, carry on trade and commerce honestly and make use of the wealth for favourable deeds. They shouldn't be greedy, selfish and corrupt.[47] Based on these descriptions, one may comment that there was perhaps some willingness in the trading society of the *AV* time to help the Paṇīs to overcome their sins or afflictions.

DĀSAS AND DASYŪS

The words *Dāsa* and *Dasyū* occur in the *AV-saṁhitā* as in other *Vedas*. Very often, they refer to a particular type of the common people who were engaged in laboursome work in ancient India. The etymological references will suffice to designate the human races indicated by both these terms.

Yāskācārya, the author of *Nirukta* which is an etymological text on the *Veda*s and one of the *Vedāṅga*s, interprets the term *Dāsa* as *dāso dasyate:* (2.17) whereas its critic Durgācārya explains the word as *dāsaḥ karmkaraḥ* (2.17.1), meaning, a person engaged in laboursome work. V.S. Apte in his modern dictionary suggests the meaning of the word as a worker occupied some work. So, we may conclude that the term *Dāsa* designates the common people working on the agricultural farm or cattle-farm, etc.

Another word *Dasyū* referred to in *Nirukta* as *Dasyumagnirja-ghanvāṁ* (7.23) means the extinguisher of the sacred fire. Durgācārya comments on *abhidasyum* as *dāsayitāram*, the beings who force some one to serve as Dāsa. V.S. Apte (p. 806) has also interpreted this term as the evil-beings, the demons, who were supposed to be harassing the human beings. Those *Asuras* — the *Piśāccas* or goblins, the wizards or magicians and the *Kimīdinas*, the robbers comprising the Dasyu community show some agreement with the non-Āryan native community of the *AV* time. Thus, as per the Āryan Vedic-text interpretations, the Dāsas were the common people or the masses defeated by the Āryans and employed on laboursome tasks such as agriculture, cattle breeding, etc. whereas Dasyūs were the foemen of the Āryans coming in their way of invasion.

The Dāsa-community of the *AV* time, as indicated in the verses from the text, was tormented by their enemies:

> *vāvṛdhānaḥ śavásā bhūryójāḥ śatrúrdāsāyá bhiyasáṃ dadhāti* I
> *avyánacca vyanacca sasni saṃ té navanta prabhṛ́tā madéṣu* I I

The Dāsa is afraid of the strong, wild, attacking foemen. Otherwise, they with their living and non-living beings used to reside together with due happiness.

The Āryans were perhaps always preoccupied with keeping the Dāsas under their control. The rules and regulations laid down by Varuṇa, the head of the Āryan religion and culture, were applicable equally to both the Dāsas and Āryans but the Āryan invaders wanted the Dāsas to have a downtrodden status, as is clear in the following verse:

> *ekaṃ rajása enā paro anyadástyenā para ekéna durṇaśáṃ cidarvāk* |
> *tatté vidvānvárunạ pra brávīmyadhovácasaḥ Paṇayó bhavantu nīcairdāsā upá sarpantu Bhūmím* ||

> Owing to the affliction, somewhat is on either side of the soil whereas definitely another is on the other because of the difference. O Varuṇa, you are knowing what it is. I invoke you loudly that the Paṇis would pass downwards keeping quiet while the Dāsas would go creeping on the Earth.

The Dāsas had to work hard either on the agricultural farm or on the cattlefarm. The *AV* does not mention their wages or payment of any livestock to them by their masters. Women were, as a practice or fashion, possessed as servants in the household. They also worked during the harvest season. A verse from the *AV* states:

> *yádasyāḥ palpúlanaṃ śakṛ́d dāsī samasyáti* |
> *tato'párūpaṃ jāyate tasmādavyéṣyadenásaḥ* ||

> (The cow) Only when the lady servant sweeps away the cowdung completely, wins over as having somewhat distinct feature making you free from all the afflictions.

They were used for some other purposes that required unbridled cruelty as, for example, courtesans poisoning warriors on the front:

> *Uruguláyā duhitā jātā dāsyasíknyā* |
> *pratáṅkáṃ dadruṣīṇāṃ sarvásāmarasaṃ viṣam* ||

The daughter of Urugulā employed as courtesan of Asiknī, scare away the highly poisoning performance of all other maidens.

As far as the *AV-saṁhitā* is concerned, it is repeatedly invoked in the verses that the misfortune of being a slave — the Dāsya — might not even touch a person. The persons employing others as slaves are violently cursed as in the following verse:

yo naḥ svo yo aráṇaḥ sajāta uta niṣṭayo yo asmān ábhidāsáti ।
Rudraḥ śáravya'yaitān mamāmitrān vi vídhyatu ।।

He, who may be ours or from others, may be from our caste by birth or a foreigner moulding us as slaves, Rudra would hurt my such foemen with his arrows.

It was expected that the harassers of common people, who employed them as Dāsas, would have their wildness reduced by Indra and would be stripped of their livestock and kicked out of their residential places by him. The Apāmārga plant and Añjanamaṇī — an amulet — were invoked through magic spells to ruin such oppressors:

vibhindatī śataśákhā vibhindannáma te pitā ।
pratyagvi bhíndhi tvaṃ taṃ yo asmān ábhidāsáti ।।

O, you Apāmārga plant, having branches split into hundreds in number, possessing father powerful in splitting it would immediately blast them who employ us as Dāsas.

All these evidences from the *AV* text clearly show the practice of imposing slavery — Dāsya — on the common people by the Āryan invaders of the time.

OTHERS

Some people from ancient India earned their living by hunting and were called Pāśin due to their use of snares as tools. They were offensive travellers catching cows and other domestic animals on snares. The people who skilfully pierced the butt and lived on robbery are named Śvaghnī. There were Niṣādas of the Pancajana sector. The Kirātas — Bhillas — the foresters lived upon forest means. They were put under a single category and labelled *Vanin* or *Vanecara* due to their residence in the forests. The *AV* refers to a tribe as *Itarajana*. Perhaps, they were not engaged in any particular deed or business and were attributed with no special achievements. The people apart from those in settled societies or the scheduled tribes may be, therefore, viewed as *Itarajana*.[48] Prof. Benjamin Walkar says of these foresters: "Their knowledge of herbal-lore was proverbial and passages in the *AV* relate how the Āryans used to purchase the herbal drugs from the kirāta-girl in exchange for mats and skins".[49]

AV describes the nature of some natives as 'vehemently touching the sky' and 'attacking violently.' It refers to them as 'Yātudhānas,' 'Muradeos' and 'Śiśnadeos'. A term, 'Parivargya' is also applied to natives.

By and large, we can see that the *AV* terms all the people other than Āryans as non-Āryans. Some from those tribes possessed a war-like nature but overall a lot of things were shared such as occupation. Perhaps the natives driven out by the Āryans migrated in all directions of the Indian region. They might have had to struggle with the natives therein before settling, preserving their own characteristics distinct from those of the Āryans. The *AV* established itself originally among these natives and it exhalts many of their customs. Thus, one can penetrate the common life of all people in general in the Vedic times only through this *Saṃhitā*.

References

1. 3.10.11.
2. *Hindu-World*, Vol. 1, p. 300.
3. *Atharvaveda kā Subodha-bhāṣya, bhāga* 1-4-9.3.9.
4. 9.3.4.
5. *Hindu-World*, Vol. 1, p. 102.

6. *Atharvaveda kā Subodha-bhāṣya, bhāga* 1-4-9.3.20.
7. *Saṃskṛtisugaṃdha*, p. 229.
8. *Atharvaveda kā Subodha-bhāṣya, bhāga* 1-4-7.81.1.
9. 7.60, 3.12, 14, 9.3, 1.2, 7.81, 9.6, 7.6.
10. 4.34.5.
11. 4.34, 9.5, 10.9, 10, 3.29, 11.1, 3, 12.3, 14.3, 20.71, 3.34, 6.69, 70, 10.6, 15.9, 7.58.
12. *Hindu-World*, Vol. 1, p. 309.
13. *Atharvaveda kā Subodha-bhāṣya, bhāga* 1-4-2.13.2.
14. 8.2.16, 2.13, 14.2, 13.3, 15.2, 20.30, 32, 8.2.
15. 20.128.7.
16. 19.57.5.
17. An Āryan Invasion — A Myth, p. 168.
18. *Atharvaveda kā Subodha-bhāṣya, bhāga* 1-4-8.2, 20.128, 19.57, 20.130, 20.127-136, 12.1, 10.9, 10.
19. 7.50.1.
20. 7.109.1.
21. 4.38, 7.50, 109, 6.118.
22. 4.18, 5.14, 4.34, 5.17, 7.90, 8.6, 20.96.
23. 5.7.8.
24. 3.1.5, 3.2.1.
25. 4.17.5, 5.6, 2.19, 3.18, 4.22, 45, 47, 7.9, 59.
26. 1.16.4.
27. 2.14.1.
28. 4.7.1.
29. 2.24, 1.16, 4.3, 4.21, 7.75, 4.36, 14.1, 19.47, 49, 50, 4.3, 1.7, 8.8, 18.2, 1.8, 4.3, 5.29, 8.4, 19.44, 47, 2.14, 4.7.
30. 1.28.4.
31. 1.7, 16, 28, 2.24, 1.19, 4.36, 7.90, 109, 8.3, 4, 19.28, 49.
32. *Atharvavedāce Marāṭhī Bhāṣāṃtara-Prastāvanā*, p. 1.
33. *Atharvaveda kā Subodha-bhāṣya, bhāga* 1-3.17.
34. *Lokasāhitya Āṇi Lokasaṃskṛtī*, pp. 175, 125, 126. *Mahārāṣṭra: Lokasaṃskṛti Va Sāhitya*, p. 102.
35. *Atharvaveda kā Subodha-bhāṣya, bhāga* 1-4 — 6.50.
36. *Marāṭhī cenema — Kasa Kāya Pāṭil Bara Hāya Kā?*
37. *Atharvaveda kā Subodha-bhāṣya, bhāga* 3-7.38.

38. *Lokasāhitya Āṇi Lokasaṃskṛtī*, p. 27.
39. *Atharvaveda kā Subodha-bhāṣya, bhāga* 3-8.2.17.
40. *Mahārāṣṭra: Lokasaṃskṛtī Va Sāhitya*, p. 175.
41. *Atharvaveda kā Subodha-bhāṣya, bhāga* 4-127-136.
42. *Lokasāhitya Āṇi Saṃskṛtī*, p. 8.
43. *Atharvaveda kā Subodha-bhāṣya, bhāga*, 3-8.1, *bhāga*, 4-17.2, 1.
44. *Mahārāṣṭra: Lokasaṃskṛtī Va Sāhitya*, pp. 51, 56.
45. *Atharvaveda kā Subodha-bhāṣya, bhāga* 1-4-2.9.2.
46. 5.11.7.
47. 5.11, 20.91, 93, 25, 128.
48. 17.1, 20.34, 14.4, 19.2, 8.10, 9.7, 10.10.
49. *Hindu-World*, Vol. 1, p. 555.

4

Feminine Life

THE position and status of the Indian woman has seen variations in different periods of history. Historians and sociologists have pondered over this from different angles and drawn confusing and even contradictory conclusions. For instance, in the Vedic literature, scholars on the one hand exhalt the life of the woman and revere her as a lady seer or even female deity and on the other hand, sketch a picture where she is ensnared in slavery. Let us study the life of the woman as apparent in the *AV* and see what kind of conclusions can be drawn.

Birth of a Girl

It is noted that generally all the people expect a boy from a pregnant woman. The *AV* is not an exception to it. The people of the *AV* time, it is seen, were not in want of a girl. A deep desire to have a boy is invoked in the hymns of the *AV*. The *AV* seer Brahmā says:

> *pumā́ṃsaṃ pu̱traṃ jánaya̱ taṃ pumā̱nanú jāyatām* |
> *bhavā́si pu̱trāṇā́ṃ mā̱tā jā̱tānā́ṃ ja̱nayā́śca̱ yān* ||
>
> Please give birth to a male child and then the boys should be born from you one after the another. You would be the mother of the boys (only) who have taken birth and of those who have to take birth from you.[1]

It is invoked that all the medicinal plants and the potential plants might pour the juices and extracts of their fruits and seeds into the body of a boy taking birth and he should be beautiful, strong and stout with all the good qualities. The mother would acquire a holy seat like that of a cow with her calf and she would be rendered free from barrenness owing to the birth of her male child. As the boy keeps up the position etc. of his mother, she should be auspicious to him. It is invoked in an *AV* verse:

> O lady, the creepers having sky and earth as their father and mother and originated from the sea, may offer you divine medicines so you may deliver a son.

In the *Śaunakīya Saṁhitā* of the *AV*, Brahmā beseeches Soma, Tvaṣṭā, Savitṛ and Prajāpati to give a son to his woman. It is righteously advised that a man meet with his wife between the holy fig tree — the Aśvattha — and the *mimosa suma* — the *Śami* — for having a male child. Potentially, the power of producing a son is only in the male body, as it is said in the *AV*. Prajāpati, Anumati and Sinīvālī invoke that there should be boys only in their family and the girls might be born elsewhere. This phenomenon is designated as *Straiṣūya* in the following verse:

> *Prajāpátiranúmatiḥ Sinīvālya'cīklṛpat* ।
>
> *staiṣūyamanyatra dadhat pumáṃsamu dadhadiha* ।।
>
> Prajāpati, Anumati and Sinīvālī argued that the female foetus may be possessed elsewhere while (the pregnant woman from their family) should bear only the foetus of the male-child there.[2]

The theory implying the *Straiṣūya* was a question-mark before the life of a woman. Brotherless maidens were hated everywhere in the society.[3]

The father trembled with fear when a girl was born in his family. Only the boys were allowed to enjoy freedom. On the occasion of putting on the holy bangles before delivery it was invoked that the pregnant woman may carry a male child. Aditī and Maryādā, a couple of head-ladies cooking rice to prepare cake for oblation in the *Brahmaudanasava,* a large sacrifice for the Supreme Rice, imagine the birth of a male child from a pregnant woman in their family. The ladies were meant to take more care of their brave sons, brothers and husbands than any of the female members of the family. It was expected that the earth would be rich with milk for their sons. The father got his daughter married and she entered her husband's house to produce healthy sons only, as it is described in a verse. The grandfather and the grandmother are expected to enjoy their retired life in playing and laughing with their grandsons. Only sons are said to possess the right of religious worship. The golden gang of only the sons should be present in the family, as it is recited in the following part of a verse:

sā̱dhuṃ pu̱traṃ hira̱ṇyayám । 20.129.5[4]

Not only the man but also the woman expressed her desire from the very bottom of her heart for brave and strong sons and not girls. The women, it seems, were in a race to capture the 'holy' seats as mothers of sons or as sisters of great warriors! How selfishly it is invoked that only sons should take birth in one's family whereas the girls should be born elsewhere! Prajāpatī, the god of creation and an unfortunate father of a female-child, was represented in a very pitiful condition as regards status at the time of the *AV.*

From Childhood to Marriage

The *Śaunakīya Saṁhitā* of the *AV* describes the childhood of the woman of the time. If the girls took birth one after the other in a family and they did not have any brothers, they were looked down upon everywhere in the society. A physician compares such girls with leaked blood-vessels:

a̱mūryā yantí yo̱ṣitó hi̱rā lohítavāsasaḥ ।
a̱bhrātáraḥ iva jā̱maya̱stiṣṭántu ha̱tavárcasaḥ ।।

These (flowing blood-vessels) should stop (and remain stand-

> still) like those young, splendid girls passing by wearing red clothes but having no brothers (and therefore) lacking lustre.[5]

The language in this verse indicates the insult and guilt heaped upon these young girls.

However, in some verses, we strangely meet with loving words uttered towards the girls. Atharvan invokes in *Varaṇamaṇisūkta* — the hymn for worshipping amulet:

> *yathā̱ yaśáḥ ka̱nyā'yā̱ṃ yathā̱'smintsaṃbhṛ́te̱ rathé* |
>
> *e̱vā mé Vara̱ṇo ma̱ṇiḥ kī̱rtiṃ bhūti̱ṃ niyácchatu̱ tejásā ma̱*
>
> *samúkṣatu̱ yaśásā̱ samánaktu mā* ||
>
> The worshipping amulet would offer me the fame and prosperity as is there in anyone's daughter and as is there in the chariot fully equipped with these and ready to ride on.[6]

A girl owing to her good character achieves fame all around for her father's family rich with livestock. The girl should maintain her purity and auspicious youth up to her marriage — the *Brahmacarya* — as it is advised in the *AV* for, it provides the girl an opportunity to have a good partner in married life. The lustrous energy possessed by a girl is compared by the *AV* with that in a brave man, horse, deer and elephant.

It is but natural that a girl desires to enjoy her delightful period of childhood in her father's house. Tvaṣṭā, the divine fashioner, built a beautiful chariot for his daughter and showed her the threefold world in it. On the beauty, exhilarating youth and puberty of the girls, the *AV* says:

> *suprápā̱ṇā cá veśa̱ntā re̱vānt supratídiśyayaḥ* |
>
> *suyámyā ka̱nyā'kalyā̱ṇī to̱tā kalpéṣu sa̱mmitā́* ||
>
> Only a fortunate person can achieve, after millions of years, the houses attached with wells full of sweet water to drink, rich hosts offering a lot of gifts, a person having a pleasing

policy and a girl possessing good character with puberty in young age.[7]

The *AV* mentions the power of understanding and the co-operative nature of the girls as special qualities and also marks the events of joking and jesting in their life before marriage.[8]

Marriage Settlement

Marriage is rather a revolutionary change that happens in the life of a girl whereby she acquires a new status — in her husband's family and community. Perhaps, the marriage system came into existence owing to the limitations on the union of the man and woman. The concept of marriage, however, changed along with cultural changes in the Indian society and many types of marriages were introduced. Many details regarding the rite of marriage have been mentioned in the hymns of the *AV* especially in Book XIV.

With marriage, the married man and woman legalize their living with each other till the end of their lives. Therefore, the community tries its best to settle all the terms and conditions of the marriage before the wedding. But there is some partiality in case of these settlements and the particularities of the bride-party are verified more strictly than those of the bridegroom-party. The Ātharvaṇa seer advises only a girl on behalf of the expectations of the bridegroom, asking her to behave courteously in her father's house, etc. She is to assist the husband in achieving success like a tree assisting in the making of a garland of flowers. The young girl must be standstill in her father's house like the line of mountains on the earth. She should be with tranquil mind, worshipping *Brahmacarya*. The girl of the *AV* time was strictly indoored in her father's house. She was told that the prohibitions were put on her by Yama — the god of religion — and she should reside in her father's house until decorated with auspicious ornaments, a marriage crown and a holy cream with *Sindūra* at the time of marriage. She is safe in her father's custody as a treasure locked in a box, a surgeon assures a patient in the following *AV* verse:

> *a̱nta̱ḥ ko̱śamíva jā̱myo'pí nahyāmi te̱ bhagáṃ* I (1.14.4)
>
> Splendid girls are as if a treasure safely deposited in their father's house, sealed and, I am going to lock your wound like that.

The girl to be wedded was to be beautiful. A girl without inauspicious fatal marks on her arms and legs and a bad-looking hair-style and practising no ridiculous purificatory rites through her behaviour celebrates herself as a queen-bride. A girl with slim legs as those of a deer, having teeth like those of a bull, walking like a cow and talking with an unpleasant voice was not at all accepted as a bride. Here we may point out that unfortunately, as such, the Indian women possessing inauspicious marks on the body have been blamed everywhere in their community. Bad-looks and an unhealthy practice of walking and talking are the omens that have severely affected the woman's life right from the ancient time of the *AV*.

Some minimum expectations from the bridegroom, such as an eagerness on his part for the marriage rite and his having no other wife, have been invoked in the *AV*.

The Ātharvaṇa seer suggests a very simple and practical way to calculate the age of youths suitable for marriage. When the young boys and girls participating in the marriage-ceremony of their friends begin to think of their own marriage, then the proper time for their wedding has arrived. The following verse, for instance, says:

> *aśrámadiyamáryamanna̱nyāsā̱ṃ samánaṃ ya̱tī* I
>
> *a̱ṅgonva'ryamanna̱syā a̱nyā̱ḥ samána̱māyáti* I I
>
> O Aryaman, the Sungod of the household, this (young girl) going to attend the marriage festival of someone (from her companions) is too nervous. So, O god, her marriage must be arranged soon after the girl's wedding being held now.[9]

The marriages were proposed as it is stated in the marriage hymn and *Pativedana-sūkta* — the hymn on the rite of addressing the bridegroom. The father of a young girl, along with his kinsmen, approached the house of a young boy. The *AV* seer describes how he is welcomed to the house:

> *a̱gacchata̱ āgatastha̱ nāmá gṛhṇāmyāya̱taḥ* ।
> *Indrásya Vṛtra̱ghno vánve Vāsa̱vasyá Śa̱takrátoḥ* ॥
>
> Please come. Arrived, you please have a seat. I, in your honour, invite you to our Indra's house, who is the slayer of Vṛtra, has prosperity and is the performer of the hundred sacrifices.[10]

The relatives of the bride judged the politeness of the relatives of the bridegroom as well as their economic status.

In the following verse from *Brahmajāyā-sūkta* — a hymn of the Brāhmaṇa's wife — an anxiety is whether the partners in the wedding are marrying for the first time or they have already been married before:

> *u̱ta yatpatáyo̱ daśá striyāḥ pūrve̱ abráhmaṇāḥ* ।
> *Bra̱hmā ceddhasta̱magráhītsa e̱va patírekadhā* ॥
>
> If a woman had married with ten men before but with those who were other than Brāhamaṇs and now if a Brāhmaṇa wishes to receive her hand in marriage, then, he only would achieve a right as her husband.[11]

This indicates that there was a custom of remarriage in the period of *AV.* A Brāhmaṇa could marry many brides, that is, many times, willingly and a Brāhmaṇa bride would not want to marry a man other than a Brāhmaṇa, as is mentioned in the *AV.*

To get married before an elder brother was supposed to be an inauspicious omen for a bridegroom in the time of the *AV.* The expectations from a boy and a girl wedding each other are mentioned in the *Pativedana-sūkta*. The girl must be a scholar, beautiful and praiseworthy whereas the boy should be garrulous and rich. The young boy and the girl were introduced to each other with Soma, Brahmā and Aryamā as witnesses. The girl was allowed to marry her beloved bridegroom but under the supervision of her kinsmen:

> *Bhagásya nāvạmāróha pụ̄rṇāmanúpadasvatīm* ।
> *tayópạpratā́rayạ yo vạraḥ prátikạ̄mya'ḥ* ॥
>
> Please step towards the boat possessed by Bhaga, the god of prosperity and then with full confidence crossing on the boat reach up to the bridegroom that you are willing to marry.[12]

The types of marriages are mentioned in the hymn that deals with a dialogue between Yama and Yamī — the god of religion and his divine sister. Yamī introduces herself as a bride before Yama. She states that both of them have been born from Prajāpati and are made for each other. So, their father would not be blamed in any case for their union. All the deities, Gandharvas — the demi-gods — and the Apsarās — the nymphs — have been convinced regarding their marriage. She further says that if he is not willing to accept her as his bride, some other girl would certainly change his policy of keeping himself alone and he would be ready to embrace her in sexual conjugation. By and large, Yama opposes this proposal from Yamī up to the last extent and appeals that the marriage cannot be settled between a male and a female born of the same couple. It can be said from this discussion that the marriage between a brother and a sister was strictly prohibited at the time of the *AV*.

After the willingness of the boy and the girl for their wedding, the relatives, guests and friends along with the lady members were invited personally to enjoy the marriage festival:

> *ạtmānáṃ pịtaráṃ pụtraṃ pautráṃ pitāmạham* ।
> *Jạ̄yāṃ janítrīṃ mạ̄tarạṃ ye priỵāstānupáhvaye* ॥
>
> We invoke with invitations to our father, son, grandson and grandfather along with wife, mother giving birth and those who are ever lovable to us.[13]

Marriage-ceremony

The details regarding the marriage-ceremony are given in Book XIV of the *Śaunakīya Saṁhitā.* It cannot be said that the marriage function at the time of this *Veda* was celebrated in the same manner as at present but keeping in mind the series of rites we perform under this function, it is possible to describe how the ceremony was enjoyed even at that ancient time.

The marriage-ceremony was initiated with a holy bath. The bride and the bridegroom both had to take bath on the square-seat made of wood placed in the midst of all the people invited for the marriage festival. The bath might have been taken after an oil massage and the sacred fire was invoked to wash out all the evils and magical spells along with the dirt from the body, clothes, bedding and cart:

> *yad dúṣkṛtaṃ yacchamálaṃ vivāhe váhatau ca yat* ।
> *tat sáṃbhalasyá kambale mṛjmahé duritaṃ vayam* ।।
>
> On the occasion of taking bath before marriage, we wash out all the evil deeds along with the dirt from the cart and that from the bedding and clothes with affliction if any.[14]

The hair was dressed in style and the marriage dress was decorated in the fashion of that time. Aśvinau — the twingods — are specially invoked to perform this deed. They beautifully did the make-up of the bride with fragrant powders and cosmetics of various kinds and dressed her up in colourful clothes. The dresses of the couple were smooth to touch and pleasant to put on. The bride was cleverly dressed in smooth clothes with a folding in the front. The women used to weave a precious marriage-*sārī* for the bride-to-be.

The bride was brought to the place of marriage either by *Meṇā* — the *Pālakhī* — or in the cart or chariot decorated beautifully:

> *Sūryāyá vahatuḥ prāgátsavitā yamavāsṛ́jat* ।
> *Maghāsú hanyante gāvaḥ Phalgúnīṣu vyúhyate* ।।

> The Sūryā's chariot initiated by Savitṛ went on ahead (to participate in her marriage). The cows have been slaughtered (for sacrifice) on Maghā constellation and then the marriages have been arranged on Phalgunīs.[15]

The auspicious time-interval between the month of Māgha and Phālguna in Hindu calendar might be mentioned in this verse. There was a fashion of offering gratitude towards each other by both the parties before marriage. The function was celebrated in the *paṇḍāl* for the marriage. The family priests uttered the verses in praise of the Vedic deities from Agni — the sacred fire — to Bhaga, the god of prosperity. The people from the bride's party willingly offered some part of their cattle, gold, etc. to their female child to help her in settling. However, giving of presents to the bridegroom has not been seen even at the time of the *AV*. But the above-mentioned rite cannot be interpreted as the origin of the custom of dowry because this developed later on, perhaps in the period of the *Dharmaśāstra*s — the religious texts.

A number of verses from Book XIV are rich with precious advice by parents for the newly-wedded couple especially the bride. The husband and wife should conjugate to produce lustrous children like the sun and the moon. They should try to achieve a lot of wealth and cattle. The Aryaman — the sungod — is implored to provide a better household and the couple is advised to go round the sacred fire on incantation of holy verses employed for the benefit of the husband and wife in gold, water, time and happiness. During this rite, the bridegroom receives the right hand of the bride in his right hand in front of the sacred fire, invoking:

> *gṛhṇāmí te saubhagatvāya hastaṃ mayā patyā́ jaradáṣṭirya thāsáḥ* ।
> *Bhagó Aryamā Sávitā Purándhirmahyáṃ tvādurgārhá-patyāya devāḥ* ॥

> (O my dear wife) I am receiving your hand in that of mine for my prosperity. Please reside with me — your husband —

> till old age. The gods Bhaga, Aryamā, Savitṛ and Purandhi — the towngoddess — have given you to me for performing sacrifices on the Gārhapatya Agni — the sacred fire in the household.[16]

The bridegroom had to announce that the bride has an equal right as the head of their family. Both of them pledged that they shall live together for hundreds of years. The bridegroom was warned in respect of his duties for his family, kin and society. The bride was expected to come to the residence of her husband with good fortune. Her arrival was not to cause any accident to her kinsmen, cattle and her husband. She was also not to cause any damage in her own life. It is mentioned in the *AV* that the newly-wedded couple might help each other to have a good living, protection and healthy life in favour of their society. Both of them should be ambitious towards the status as the head of the common people from their community. The common society of the *AV* expected the newly-married couple to reside on this very earth along with all others:

> *ihaiva staṃ mā vi yaúṣṭaṃ viśvamāyurvya'śnutam* |
> *krīḍántau putrairnaptṛ́bhirmodámānau svastakau* ||
>
> Please reside here in this world. Don't be apart from each other. Enjoy the full duration of life, playing with sons and grandsons with pious delight.[17]

One may deny the above description of marriage-rite between Soma and Sūryā, a divine couple, owing to the fact that the narration is concerned with the classes and not the masses — the masses cannot celebrate the event on an elaborate scale. But a man, even a commoner, always thinks of enjoying the religious rites and cultural ceremonies in a grand manner even though he would have to hire a loan for this purpose. After all, marriage rites are common for all. Whether from the divine community, or the classes or masses, a member approaches marriage once in a life. Therefore there is the attempt to enjoy every event including the marriage festival to the ultimate satisfaction. Therefore, the above objection cannot be sustained.

The marriage-hymns from Book XIV and many other verses contain information about the status offered to the ancient Indian woman at the time of the *AV*. In a homage paid to the couple, the Indian lady along with her husband is compared with the wheels of a chariot to indicate her equal share. It is indeed in the period of this *Veda*, when work was supposed to be worship, that the members of the family had to reside jointly gathering gems of happiness from wherever possible:

> *anúvrataḥ pitụḥ pụtro mātrā bhávatụ saṃmánāḥ* ।
> *jāyā patyẹ madhúmatīṃ vācáṃ vadatu śantịvām* ।।
>
> The son might behave accordingly with his sire and willingly pay homage to his mother. The wife should speak to her husband sweetly — as is nectar — with due peacefulness.[18]

The charms pertaining to the health of the family were performed to scare away the jealousy between brothers and sisters. How solemnly the *AV* seer announces that they should have lunch together and quench their thirst from the same waterhouse:

> *sạmānī prạpā sạha vó'nnabhāgaḥ sámāne yoktré sạha vó yunajmi* ।
> *sạmyañcọ'gniṃ sáparyatārā nābhímivābhitáḥ* ।।
>
> As the spokes of the chariot-wheel connecting the hub surround it overall, in common, our waterhouse might be common for all of us. I must share the part of my food with all other mouths equally and our sacred fire might be common for all.[19]

Problems Before a Newly-Married Wife

Innumerable hostile magical songs and hymns employed in the charms pertaining to women's rites in the *AV* in particular submit a substantial account of the vigorous problems faced by women during the *AV* period. Strangely enough, the benedictory hymns such as marriage-rites, the rite associated with depositing of a child and others indicate the many calamities that arose in the life of the ancient Indian woman.

A lady married newly had some problems regarding the etiquettes and religious or mythical customs in practice in her husband's family. Sometimes her husband's relatives looked at her suspiciously as if she would employ some magical spells to take away her husband from his parents and settle in a different place:

> *parā́ dehi śāmu̱lyaṃ'bra̱hmabhyo̱ vi bhā́jā̱ vasú* ।
> *kṛ̱tyaiṣā pa̱dvatī bhū̱tvā jā̱yā viśáte̱ patím* ।।

> O my boy married newly, scare away this silky-clothes and enjoy prosperities achieved from your own kins. This vixen employed by your wife, taking paramour of your bride, enters into the body of one's own husband.[20]

And it is seen very often that some blind faiths and mischievous customs were followed by the members of the patriarchal type of society — for example, thinking it to be inauspicious when even a piece of women's clothing is put on by men — that degraded the status of the Indian woman even in the ancient time of the *AV*.

The Woman's Work

The woman of the *AV* time had to contribute much work in her big joint family. She had to maintain the house, contribute labour on the farmhouse and, in addition, look after the herds of cattle. The wife of a cattle-breeder had the responsibility of milking the cows along with some laboursome work of food-gathering. Two great head-ladies, Diti and Aditi, are mentioned as busy in pounding the rice, grinding and winnowing the foodgrains and respectfully executing the right of distributing the food among the members of their joint-families. The ladies were to decorate the dishes, settle the remains after lunch was over and, moreover, clean the containers. The Apasarās are invoked for a better household:

vicinvatīmākirantīmapsarām sādhudevinīm |
galahé kṛtāni gṛhṇānāmápsarām tāmiḥ húve ||

Here I worship with oblations the splendid, lustrous Apsarā — the nymph holding the duties from our houses.[21]

The women undergoing the purificatory rite were appointed, as it is described in the text, for supplying the water and cooking the sacrificial food. They were busy with the selection of the richest variety from the rice, rinsing it with water and cooking it, filtering it and covering it with a light cloth under pressure. They cut the vegetables and cleaned and made it ready for cooking. Some of the women applied mud on outer sides of the huge vessels for cooking and the pans were supplied with a handful of butter before being placed on the fireplace. The ladies were also to supply water to the site of the plots under construction for altars and also to the cattlefarms. The ladies were experts in weaving and spinning and decorated the clothes for their family-members. They were involved in the work of splitting the *ratan* to prepare the mats, gathering the forest-means, dyeing clothes and drawing colourful designs on them.[22]

At the time of the *AV*, the ladies were occupied with the laboursome work and with not even a little of intellectual work. We can conclude that approximately fifty per cent of the ancient Indian society was not assigned the duty of invocation of holy hymns, offering oblations into the sacred fire or any other dignified work as such in rituals.

Motherhood

The woman achieves her appropriate status in life, as it is supposed, only when she attains motherhood. The birth of a child especially a son was treated as an event of great importance at the time of the *AV*. To bear many children was seen as of higher status at that time. The Indians in fact have celebrated motherhood applying even a divine touch; at the same time very basic and practical views on this subject can be culled from the Vedic texts especially the *AV*. This *Veda* represents more scientific information than any other ancient text on subjects related to motherhood such as pregnancy including diseases arising in the period of pregnancy, delivery and maternal love.

PREGNANCY

In benedictions from the *AV* song VI.17, the pregnancy of a woman is described irrespective of the sex of the child. The pregnancy of a woman is highly extolled here and she is compared to the Mother Earth:

> *yatheyaṃ Pṛthivī Mahī bhūtānāṃ garbhámādadhe* |
> *evā té dhriyatāṃ garbho anu sūtuṃ savítave* ||
>
> As the great Mother Earth bears the foetus of all beings (O Lady), bear a child to deliver easily.

Diseases Related to Pregnancy

The notion that various kinds of germs and insects cause diseases in the pregnant woman developed in the period of the *AV*. Insects bearing names like Darṇāmā, Aliṃśa, Sarka, Kaka, Malimluca and Palija are said to possess germs. With long hairs and horns, they come in contact with the pregnant woman and bite her. The worms named Baja smell the inner organs of the woman, cut through to consume the muscles and even cause barrenness. Kusūla, Kukṣila, Kakubha, Kasuma, Striya, Kakumdha, Kakūrabha and Kṛtti are described as species of insects hiding themselves among branches of trees within forests. Buzzing with their feathers, they bite the child severely. The mosquitoes keeping themselves away from heat and sunlight are said to bite the pregnant woman and cause blood diseases. The insects dwelling in the kitchen badly affect the embryo of the woman. Therefore according to the *AV*, the insects and the germs should be destroyed where and when they are found. At any cost, care should be taken to safeguard the mental and physical health of the woman during the period of pregnancy. The Kimīdinas, as paramours, cause bad dreams in this period and disturb the pregnant woman mentally while she is in sleep. So, they are to be driven out from the women's compartments.[23]

DELIVERY

In the verses of the *AV*, Atharvan extolls the act of delivering a child and compares it to a ritual:

> *vaṣáṭ te Pūṣannas̠mintsūtávaryam̠ā Hotā́ kṛṇotu ve̠dhāḥ* ।
> *sistrátā̠ṃ nāryar̠taprájātā̠ vi parvā́ṇi jihatā̠ sūta̠vā ú* ।।
>
> O Pūṣan, the Sungod, I offer you oblations invoking 'Vaṣaṭ'. Aryamā would act as Hotṛ in this ritual of delivery. This woman originated in the universal order — the *Ṛta* would let loose her organs for delivery.[24]

The Ātharvaṇa physician advises the mother on the occasion of her delivery. She should enrich the embryo, to make it free from her stomach. She should not exert pressure on the muscular, colloid and nervous part of her body. The membrane on the foetus would go apart, the orifice of the uterus would open, the veins connected to the foetus would lie loose and the auspicious mother would give birth to a child easily. The carrier connecting the foetus to the body of the mother should be protected properly from dogs, etc. and should be buried in the soil with proper ritual. A time-interval of ten months has been specified by the *AV* for the proper growth of the embryo and for its easy delivery.

MATERNAL LOVE

Maternal love can hardly be described with any limitations to its greatness. All the conceptions of love, mineness, compassion and maternal love have originated only in the heart of a mother. The mother is only there to have her child on her lap and to pardon its offences. In litanies recited through the verses in the *AV*, we find the mother praying for the long life of a hundred years for her child. The all-pervading nature of the great mother, Aditi is invoked in the following verse:

> *Dyauṣṭvā́ pi̠tā Pṛ́thi̠vī mā̠tā jarā-mṛ́tyuṃ kṛṇutā̠ṃ*
> *saṃvidā̠ne* ।

yathā jīvā Aditerupasthe Prāṇāpānābhyāṃ gupitaḥ śatam Himāḥ ||

As the living beings have hidden themselves with the breathing air along with controlling excretion one, on the lap of Aditi, Dyau — the sky — your father, and Earth — the mother — would make known to you old-age and death, approaching after hundreds of winters.[25]

It is the mother who can build the character of her child entirely and would achieve merit for its strong and stout health. The motherland is highly praised too along with one's own mother in *AV-saṁhitā* for, she also shows her love for her offsprings. How noble is her act of having her dear child on her lap even at the end of its life:

vidmosvāsya mātraṁ Pṛthivīṃ bhūrivarcasam.[26]

BARRENNESS

Real and imaginary, both types of reasonings regarding the barrenness in woman, have been discussed in the *AV-saṁhitā*. Scientifically — in a sense somewhat near to it — the text designates a certain breed of germs that create this defect in the woman's body. On the other hand, wild curses uttered through incantations result in this condition in the co-wife, as the text of the *AV* interprets. The spell employed through the plant, Apāmārga shows the healing property of the herb and its curing the woman of barrenness:

kṣudhāmāraṃ tṛṣṇāmāramagotāmanapatyatām |
Apāmārga tvayā vayaṃ sarvaṃ tadapa mṛjmahe ||

O Apāmārga-plant, I would like to ward off the omens effecting hunger, thirst, mental-shock and barrenness in this woman.[27]

Matriarchy

Many a time, the information given by the *AV* hymns regarding the life of the ancient Indian woman seems controversial: the narration of the birth of a girl is evidance that her character was dominated and it is disheartening on the whole while invocations about the status offered to her in the marriage festival, equal rights in family life, etc. look more sublime than anything else. In some cases, there is more evidence favouring her equal, rather higher, status when compared to man's. Diti, Aditi, Anumati, Sinīvālī and Indrāṇī are accorded a bright position along with Prajāpati and Indra, etc. The *AV* seer, Mātṛnāmā recites the lustrous character of the Indian woman of his time in the songs of the *AV*. She is given high credit for possessing a divine eyesight capable of detecting magicians, goblins and even the Āryans from the Śūdras:

> *ā páśyati pratípaśyati parā́ paśyati paśyáti* |
> *divámantaríkṣamādbhūmiṃ sarvaṃ taddévi paśyati* ||
>
> O Courteous Lady, you can look forward, backward, can look beyond the things and towards the things nearby. You can observe all that is sky, atmosphere and what is there within the soil.[28]

At many places in the hymns of the *AV*, the ancient Indian woman has been glorified as the female deity who is not treated as subordinate to any of the Vedic male deities, even Indra and Agni:

> *ahaṃ Rudrebhirvasúbhiścarāmyahamādityairuta Viśva dévaiḥ* |
> *ahaṃ Mitrāvarúṇobhā bíbharmyahamíndrāgnī ahamaś vinobhā* ||
>
> I am travelling all over with Rudras — the physicians, Vasūs — the gods of the wealth and with Ādityas — the Sungods and moreover with Viśvedevās. I am holding both Mitra and Varuṇa along with both Indra and Agni.[29]

There is indeed a fair indication of the fact that the matriarchal system of family existed in some Indian regions of that time. And, after all, the woman's power would have to be recognized as far as the agro-rural society of the *AV* time was concerned as it would have been needed by the farmer at every step of his life. On this account, the names recognized as those of the lady members of the families of the time, e.g. Aditi, Diti, Sarasvatī, Devī, Nirṛtī, Anumati, Śacī, Sinīvālī, Iḍā, Kuhū, Indrāṇī, Amā, Paurṇamāsī and Durgā, etc. have been mentioned respectfully in the *AV* text.[30] Therefore, the evidence showing the ancient Indian woman in a favourable light has come from the references to families involved in agriculture and village-works and not of the warriors or priestly castes following the patriarchal family system that was seen in the colonial life of the Indian Āryans.

Polygamy

The practice of having more wives than one, polygamy and ill-practices on account of mutual jealousy originating from it affected the daily life of the women very much. Extremely wild curses are hurled through the verses of the *AV* hymns against the rival wife. The Ātharvaṇa seer, carrying out a spell on behalf of a married woman who has been disturbed by exorcisms employed by the mischievous wizard, uses an amulet of the Apāmārga plant:

> *ahamásmi sahámānātho tvamási sāsahiḥ* ।
> *ubhe sahásvatī bhūtvā sapatnī́ṃ me sahāvahai* ॥
>
> I am going to be more powerful and you originally have extreme power. Combined we with tremendous energy would overpower my co-wife, O Apāmārga-amulet![31]

A suffering lady violently arranges sorceries against the rival woman and bursts with incantations for Agni, the magical fire, asking to be discarded along with her innocent offsprings. Indrāṇī severely blames her husband Indra for his special attraction towards Vṛṣākapī and particularly towards Apālā. The people of the *AV* time believed that an effigy or a picture of the rival man or woman pierced by the arrows of the lovegod, Kāmadeva, would compel their passion for each other. And all these views and activities of the common people laid the foundation of various misbeliefs and rude customs in Indian society:

> *parạṃ yonẹravárạṃ te kṛṇomi̱ mā tvā́ prạjābhi bhụ̄nmota sūnúḥ* |
> *ạsváṃ 1̱ tvā-prájasaṃ kṛṇọmyaśmā́naṃ te api̱dhānā́ṃ kṛṇomi* ||

> I would hurt your ureter on the upper and lower part; you wouldn't be with offsprings and moreover with any child. I would scare away the breathing souls of your children and hit you with stones in addition.[32]

The woman of the *AV* time, protesting against the polygamic nature of the unfaithful husband, also sometimes violently caught hold of his clothes. The *AV* woman is rather advising the woman race in general as to how to manage relations with the males who have an excessive passionate desire of having more than one wife.

Relation Between Man and Woman

It is necessary to see what kind of treatment was accorded to a woman by her husband and other members of the family at the time of the *AV* in order to comment upon her position in the family of that time. After marriage, it is seen that women expect more attention from their husbands towards them rather than any of the other members of the family. The text of the *AV* presents its views regarding the relations between the wife and husband both on physical and psychological grounds. Innumerable verses standing midway between expiatory formulas and benedictions, the hymns employed to address the problems of the wife and husband and effect a reconciliation between them, the hymns recited for exorcism of evil demons and malicious wizards performing spells on behalf of the women's rites, could guide us to analyse the expectations of the woman from her community.

The gentleman of the *AV* time oppressed the mind of his sweetheart, wanting her to be always in his possession and fully in his command. He wants to strike and smash the mind of his beloved on the one hand and, on the other hand, requests her lovingly not to depart from him:

> *yathedaṃ Bhūmyā adhitṛṇaṃ Vātó mathāyati* ।
> *evā máthnāmi te mano yathā māṃ kāminyaso yathā mannāpágā asáḥ* ।।
>
> O my sweet-heart, I would definitely smash your mind severly as the wind strikes the delicate grass on the ground. O please, be deeply desired loving wife of mine and do not be gone as separate from me.[33]

Often too, the verses of the *AV* state that the newly married women should be polite with their husband's families. The husband, it says, would be eagerly waiting to win over his wife's body and mind, transferring all his estate to her. The wife and husband would conjugate with each other like trees and creepers, birds and Earth and also as the Earth and Atmosphere. His wife would be splendid, the man states. The passion of love and eagerness for meeting are described in a very picturesque and sublime language as in the following verse:

> *vāñchá me tanvaṃ 1 pādau vañchā-kṣyau 3 vañchá sakthyau'* ।
> *akṣyau'vṛṣaṇyantyāḥ keśā māṃ te kāména śuṣyantu* ।।
>
> Wish agreeably my body all over as with two legs and eagerly wish sweet glances from both my eyes and also wish both my laps. Your passionate eyes would have my testicles as their target and your hair would go dry on account of passionate desire for me.[34]

Each, it is stated, would feel lonely in the absence of the other and would be weakened because of separation from the other. The husband embracing his wife in his arms states that she should enter his heart lovingly then and there. Anyhow, the man of the *AV* time appears to be trying his best to please his sulking wife. He also enthusiastically requests the cows to make peace between him and his quarrelling wife. He along with his wife desires to be strong and stout as ever. He wants to share every prospect of his life with her. The couple would enjoy what is offered to them by Tvaṣṭā — the fashioner. The husband thinks about his wife more often than any of his other relations. The misfortunes would not hurt the couple, as it is invoked in many a verse. The husband and wife should be so assured about their behaviour with each other that there should not be anything private between them:

> *yadyáñjā̱yā pacáti̱ tvat pa̱raḥ pára̱ḥ patírvā jāye̱ tvat ti̱raḥ* |
> *saṃ tat sŕjethāṃ sa̱ha vā̱ṃ tadástu saṃpā̱dayántau sa̱ha lo̱kamekám* ||
>
> Whatever the wife cooks in absence of her husband and any deed that her husband performs in her absence all those would rise in the presence of them both. Achieving the fruits from the worldly life along with those from heaven, it should be gems of pious deeds that you have performed on behalf of each other.[35]

Sometimes, the husband was ready to help his wife in her work in the kitchen; then only could he expect her to assist him in his work.[36] The text of the *AV* exalts the family life of its time more rationally and fundamentally than any other contemporary religious text. And nowadays, when we are being threatened by the destruction of family life due to uncertainty, succulency and artificiality, there is much we can achieve from our great *AV*, the *Veda* of the common people!

SUBDUING BY CHARMS

Numerous spells, exorcisms with fierce incantations and sorceries full of wild curses have been employed for subduing the minds of men and women and to overpower each other in the love game. Very often too, these kinds of charms were performed owing to spiritual love for each other or because of a predominant inclination between the lovers. The practice of drawing a picture or creating a model out of clay and piercing it through with an arrow of the love-god Kāmadeva for increasing the passion of either the man or the woman was in existence in the period of the *AV*. The lover, in the following verse, shows his powerful attraction for his sweetheart:

> *uttudastvottúdatu mā dhṛ́thāḥ śayáne sve* ।
> *iṣuḥ Kāmásya yā bhīmā tayá vidhyāmi tvā hṛdi* ॥
>
> I would like to hurt your heart with the fearful arrow of the love-god so as to burst it with feelings of love for me. You would not be able to relax on your bed on account of passionate desire for me.[37]

The magical plant Apāmārga is seen as instrumental in subjecting one's wife. It was believed that demi-gods Gandharvas, taking forms of beautiful youths, tried to subdue the young beautiful ladies. Persons addicted to wine, meat and gambling were used to oppress the minds of ladies other than their own. Indeed fiercely, rather cruelly, a curse is invoked in the following verse on the unfaithful husband or lover running after a woman other than his own beloved:

> *unmádayata Maruta udántarikṣa mādaya* ।
> *Agna unmádayā tvamasau māmanúśocatu* ॥
>
> Madden him, O Maruta, O atmosphere madden him. O Agni, madden him. He might feel sorry for me.[38]

Many references on the attraction between lovers as, for example, when the lover is oppressed and captured by passionate desire for his beloved, chances of compromise between the wife and husband are lost owing to discord in the family, etc. occur repeatedly in magical rites that mention use of various plants for the purpose. Thus the following verse says:

yathā nakulo vicchidyá saṃdadhātyahiṃ punáḥ |
evā Kāmásya vicchinnaṃ saṃ dhéhi vīryāvati ||

O powerful one (Sahasraparṇī) conjoin our hearts hurt by the passionate desire of each other like the Bengal Mongoose (The Viverra Inchneumon) bites to cut down the snake and again connects its pieces to find it alive.[39]

AMOROUS DESIRE

We, however, come to know that the possessing of extravagant sexual capacity — 'The *Vājīkaraṇa*' — discussed in the *AV* developed from an amorous desire to meet with the woman on an extreme level. Many spells have been employed to accumulate such a devilish power for intercourse with the woman. In the following verse a reference is made to some animals in this context:

aśvásyāśvatarasyājasya petvásya ca |
athá ṛṣabhasya ye vājāstānasmindhéhi tanūvaśin ||

This mortal man might consume an extraordinary power for intercourse, like that in the pubert horse, mule, goat and elephant.[40]

But a person tormented by such a mischievous desire would always mount the feelings in the mind of the woman, apply violence against her and sometimes take away another's wife with him. So, he must control such an overflowing urge or maintain it to the limit of enjoying sexual conjugation with a woman.

yathāyaṃ vāho áśvinā samaiti saṃ ca vartáte |
evā māmabhi te manáḥ samaitu saṃ cá vartatām ||

My mind would be one with yours and would be equal with you in behaviour as this he-horse becomes one with his she-horse and behaves as equal with it.[41]

To enjoy sexual intercourse with more than one woman was termed *Straiṇa* in the *AV*-hymns.

> *anasthāḥ pūtāḥ pavánena śuddhāḥ śucáyaḥ śucimapi yanti lokam* |
> *naiṣā́ṃ śiśnaṃ pra dáhati Jātavédāḥ svarge loke bahu straiṇámeṣām* ||
>
> The persons standing still, pious and purified by wind, achieves delight from sexual conjugation with many beautiful ladies in heaven. The sacred fire does not dare to burn their *Śepās*, the reproductive organs.[42]

From the Brahmajāyā hymn, one may come to the conclusion that there was an evil-power in the man sufficient to take another's wife away violently. The *AV-saṁhitā* is strict against such persons. Soma having forcibly taken away the wife of Bṛhaspati returned her back to him with due respect when scolded by Varuṇa, Mitra and Saptarṣis. Moreover, it is noted that the wife of such a person does not allow him to go to bed with her.

Some fiends, e.g., violence towards the un-pubert girls to have them for satisfying one's sexual desire have also been mentioned in the *AV*:

> *yathā śepó apāyā́tai strīṣu cāsadanā́vayāḥ* |
> *avasthasyá knadīvátaḥ śaṃkurasyá nitodináḥ yadātáta mava tattánu yaduttátaṃ nitattánu* ||
>
> One who injures the *Śepās* — the reproductive organ — of unpubert girls should be arrested immediately along with those uttering bad words and possessing a subduing nature as piercing by thorns.[43]

> *vijíhīṣva lokaṃ kṛ́ṇu bandhānmúñcāsi baddhákam* |
> *yonyā́ iva pracyúto garbháḥ pathaḥ sarvān anú kṣiya* ||
>
> O person, let this world live fully. Make free the animals tied

together and make ways clear like those of foetus discharged from the uterus.[44]

Widowhood

A problem in the life of the Indian lady is the death of her husband. Very piteous is the condition of the wife and children when a man meets with death in war. This is referred to in the hymns of the *AV*. The poor lady wanders hither and thither on the war-field with her only son in her hand. The ladies with open hair cry loudly on the death of their husbands on the war-front, as it is described in the following verse:

> *pratighnānāśrúmukhī kŕdhukarṇī cá krośatu* |
> *vikeśī purúṣe hate rádite Árbude tavá* ||
>
> O fierce goddess of war, on the death of a man (as a warrior) his wife with face full of tears, smacking her ears, with hair scattered may, O lamentable one, cry loudly at you.[45]

It is but natural that the wife of a person on the war-front would expect from the bottom of her heart that her son, brother or husband remain alive in the action of war. It is often too that unfortunately some have to run here and there beating their chests, stumbling and bellowing on the demise of their parents. The hymns on *Dundubhi* — the military trumpet — and Arbudi, the goddess of war, describe the terrible plight of the family members of the warriors slain in wars. The picturesque representation of the suffering in these verses might be of the families of the rival's society, but it nevertheless hurts one's own heart. The ladies had to suffer terrible hardship because of their husbands' death in accidents or of natural causes. The woman's household loses its security within no time after the death of her partner. The funeral fire surrounds her shelter on all sides. The family of the widow is flooded with difficulties. The funeral rite is narrated in a very grievous manner. It is indeed very sorrowful to look at a lady throwing herself on the dead-body of her husband and bursting into tears and bellowing pitiably.

The woman in such an event is designated as *Satī* but this does not mean that the custom of *Satī* originated in this rite. Besides, in the following funeral hymn, the offsprings and livelihood of the unfortunate lady are referred to and she is advised to overcome her misfortune by returning to the household of the people related to her husband. The widow assured by the relatives of her late husband decides to live with them and they carry her to their shelter:

> *iyaṃ nārī́ patilokaṃ vṛṇānā ni pádyata upá tvā martya pretám* ।
> *dharmáṃ purāṇamánupālayántī tasyái prajāṃ draviṇaṃ ceha dhéhi* ।।
>
> O mortal body, this lady choosing her late husband's family bestowing on you is going to behave according to her ancient religious status and therefore, be pleased with her offering of wealth and offsprings.[46]

It is often argued by the scholars of the *AV* that the virgin widow was allowed to remarry any of the parents from her husband's side. Dr. A.H. Saḷunkhe states that there occurs not a single evidence to indicate or to support the custom of the lady accompanying the dead-body of her husband on the funeral fire to signalize her as *Satī* in that ancient period. The lady used to lie down with her dead husband on the funeral bed and then her relatives carried her home with them as it is mentioned in the verses of the *ṚV* and the *AV*.[47] Prof. Benjamin Walkar says: "Nor is there anything in the Vedas to show that it — the custom of Satī — had Vedic sanction . . . She was allowed to marry the dead-man's brother or to continue to produce children by *Niyoga*."[48]

The Problem of Abandonment

The women in the *AV* time, perhaps, had not only to face the difficulties in widowhood but there was also problem of abandonment after marriage. From the hymns employed to discard the vixen that is *Kṛtyādūṣaṇāni* we come to know, from the similes used, that the abandoned woman had to return to her father's or brother's house:

> *Śūdrakṛ́tā rājákṛtā strīkṛ́tā Brahmabhiḥ́ kṛtā* |
> *jāyā patyā́ nuttevā́ kartāram bandhvṛ́cchatu* ||
>
> A vixen employed by either a Śūdra or a king or a woman or a Brāhmaṇa should return to its employer as a wife abandoned by her husband approaches her father (or) brother.[49]

A lady abandoned by her husband might claim her right of remarriage as it is mentioned in the following verse:

> *yā pūrvaṃ patiṃ́ vittvāthānya vindate'páram* |
> *pañcaúdanaṃ ca tāvajaṃ dadā́to na vi yóṣataḥ* ||
>
> She, who was married to a man, might arrange her second marriage with another and have a sanction of not to part ways with her second husband by paying five bags of rice and a goat as a tax for expiation.[50]

References

1. 3.23.3.
2. 6.11.3.
3. 1.17, 6.11.
4. 3.23, 5.17, 25, 6.81, 11.1, 12.1, 14.1, 20.92.
5. 1.17.1.
6. 10.3.20.
7. 20.128.9.
8. 1.17, 6.22, 10.3, 11.5, 12.1, 18.1, 20.128, 10.4, 20.133, 136.
9. 6.60.2.
10. 6.82.1.
11. 5.17.8.
12. 2.36.5.
13. 9.5.30, 1.14, 1.18, 6.60, 82, 5.17, 6.112, 2.36, 18.1, 9.5, 12.5.

14. 14.2.66.
15. 14.1.13.
16. 14.1.50.
17. 14.1.22.
18. 3.30.2.
19. 3.30.6, 3.4, 8, 30.
20. 14.1.25.
21. 4.38.2.
22. 2.26, 3.24, 11.3, 12.3, 4.38, 11.1, 19.50, 3.30, 7.37, 10.7, 6.138, 10.4, 12.4.
23. 6.17.1, 5.17, 25, 6.81, 11, 17, 8.6, 20.96.
24. 1.11.1.
25. 2.28.4.
26. 2.28, 5.26, 18.3, 1.2, 5, 3.8, 5.2, 11.1.
27. 4.17.6, 3.23, 4.17.
28. 4.20.1.
29. 4.30.1.
30. 3.24, 4.20, 30, 4.30, 5.17, 24, 26, 25, 11.1, 15.6, 7.12, 18.1, 19.40, 58, 20.13, 78, 136; Aditi, 3.16, 22, 6.4, 81, 7.6, 17, 15.18; Sarasvatī, 5.28, 6.3, 7.10, 19.31, 20.125; Devī, 3.20, 6.38; Nirṛtī, 8.84; Diti, 7.7, 15.18; Anumati, 7.20; Śacī, 7.25, 20.33, 125; Sinīvālī, 7.46, 20.31; Iḍā, 7.27, 60; Kuhū, 7.47; Indrāṇī-Varuṇānī, 7.49; Amā, 7.79; Paurṇamāsī, 7.80; Durgā, 12.4.
31. 3.18.5.
32. 7.35.3, 14.1, 7.37, 4.18, 5.14.
33. 2.30.1.
34. 6.9.1.
35. 12.3.39.
36. 2.30, 5.12, 6.8, 9, 78, 89, 122, 7.36, 38, 12.3, 14.1, 18.1, 3, 4, 20.16, 17.
37. 3.25.1.
38. 6.130.4.
39. 6.139.5, 3.25, 4.18, 4.37, 6.70, 8, 130, 131, 132, 139, 7.13, 95, 20.107.
40. 4.4.8.
41. 6.102.1, 4.4, 6.72,. 102, 20.71.
42. 4.34.2.
43. 7.90.3, 4.34, 5.17, 7.90, 8.6, 20.96, 7.76.
44. 6.121.4, 7.115, 8.1, 1.18, 6.121.

45. 11.9.7.
46. 18.3.1.5.20, 8.1, 11.9, 12.1, 9.9, 11.8, 18.3.
47. *Hindu-Saṃskṛtī Āṇi Strī*, p. 95.
48. *Hindu-World*, Vol. 2, p. 461.
49. *Atharvaveda kā Subodha-bhāṣya, bhāga* 1-4, 10.1.3.
50. 9.5.27, 10.1, 18.3, 9.5.

5

The AV on Environment

AT present, the whole world is much concerned with safeguarding the environment, which has developed into an area of study with two sub-branches — natural and cultural. The foundation of this was laid in 1972 at Stockholm. The Indian scholars have very enthusiastically drawn attention towards Vedic literature, especially the *Śukla Yajurveda,* for abundant information about ancient Indian environmental thinking. However, a treasure of environmental information lies buried in the text of the *AV* mainly in the verses invoked by the common people in daily life.

The Natural Environment

The very first verse from the *Śaunakīya Saṁhitā* of the *AV* introduces the theory of natural environment with the following words:

> *ye triṣa̱ptāḥ pári̱yanti̱ viśvā́ rū̱pāṇi̱ bibhrátaḥ* ।
> *Vā̱caspati̱rbalā̱ teṣā́ṃ ta̱nvo'a̱dya dádhātu me* ।।
>
> These twenty-one energies holding all the forms surround this whole universe, Vācaspati would offer me their bodies today.[1]

The word *'Pári̱yanti̱'* from this verse indicates the environmental phenomenon, no doubt, but the mention of bodily energies is very much surprising. The five elements, the Earth, Water, Light, Wind and Atmosphere, are repeatedly mentioned in the verses of the *AV* as in the following:

> *saṃ saṃ srávantu Sindhávaḥ saṃ Vātāḥ saṃ Pátatriṇáḥ* I
> *imaṃ yajñaṃ pradivó me juṣantāṃ saṃsrāvyéṇa haviṣā́ juhomi* II
>
> The streams of water would be prosperous to us and would flow on ahead, the winds and trees would be prosperous to us. Owing to the prosperity achieved from these, I invoke them with oblations in this sacrifice which would reach to the heaven.[2]

Numerous plant-bodies possessing various colours formed by the mineral constituents present in their structures and useful for healing of diseases and as food material have been described in the *AV* as in the following verse:

> *yā babhravo yāścá śukrā rohíṇīruta praśnáyaḥ* I
> *Asíknīḥ kṛṣṇā Oṣádhīḥ sarvā́ acchāvádāmasi* II
>
> We invoke praise to the plants, chocolate in colour, bright with red and variously coloured, even black-coloured, on the bank of Asiknī and to all plants.[3]

The conjugation of the earth and atmosphere results in plant bodies as, for example, Jīvalā and Naghāriṣā. These plants possess healing properties against many diseases. Thus it is mentioned in the following verse:

> *Āpo agráṃ divyā Oṣádhayaḥ* I
> *tāste Yakṣmámenasyá 1 maṅgā́daṅgādanīnaśan* II
>
> The waters at first and then these healing plants from the Atmosphere would scare away the attack of fever from every organ of your body.[4]

The plants forming organs sweet like *ghī* and originating crops like rice, barley and Aśvattha, Darbha and Śamī growing on the mountains, plains and by the sides of lakes were known to the seers Aṅgiras. The birds and animals could also identify the potential properties of the plants, as recorded in the verses of the *AV*.

The animal being, which is the secondary constituent of the natural environment, develops its strength from divine energy evolved from nature, as the *AV* interpretes in the following verse:

> *siṃhe vyāghra uta yā pṛdākau tviṣiragnau Brāhmaṇe Sūrye vā* ।
> *Indraṃ yā devī subhagā jajāna sā na aitu varcasā saṃvidānā* ।।
>
> The goddess of prosperity who developed Indra — the king of gods with the divine energy from Lion, Tiger, Wolves, Fire, Brāhmaṇa and the Sun — would approach us with all its brilliance.[5]

Madhukaśā, a breed of cow, is very strangely described in *AV* as generating milk sweeter than the *Amṛta* owing to her structure that has developed from the sky, earth, atmosphere, sea, fire and air. The animal organs have a number of minerals and plants and these are glorified by the *AV-saṁhitā*.[6]

The rainwater as sweet as *ghī* and water from mines and rocks were understood to be a tonic and not disliked at any time. The text of the *AV* represents air as an element lying at the centre of all minerals and organic bodies of plants and animals. The word *paryāvṛta* in this renowned verse of *AV* closely resembles, in meaning, the term 'environment' in modern science:

> *Prāṇa mā mat paryāvṛto na madanyo bhaviṣyasi* ।
> *Apāṃ garbhamiva jīvase Prāṇa badhnāmi tvā mayi* ।।
>
> O the breathing air, be around me, be not apart from me. I would tie you with me to be the foetus of the waters.[7]

The *AV* seers have sometimes centralised their ideas about environment in the earth as the main source of this universe. The sand, stones and dust are said to be the mineral sources forming the earth. Thus in the following verse:

> *śilā Bhūmiraśmā pāṃsuḥ sā Bhūmiḥ saṃdhṛtā dhṛtā* ।
> *tasyai hiraṇyavakṣase Pṛthivyā akaraṃ namaḥ* ।।
>
> We salute the Earth having gold on her breast and having the rocks, stones, dust and the soil on it.[8]

The energies of the various bodies in this universe are accorded a unique status of 'Vaiśvānarī' by the *AV*.

ENVIRONMENTAL HAZARDS

There is a lot of evidence regarding natural hazards in the text of the *AV* as, for example, the impure, stored water is compared, very sensitively in fact, with harmful arrows of Rudra. High temperature, low temperature, heavy rainfall, flood, scanty rainfall, volcanic eruptions, earthquakes are mentioned as types of environmental hazards. One of the verses says:

> *atisṛṣṭo Apāṃ vṛṣabho' tisṛṣṭā Agnayo divyāḥ* ।। *rujan parirujan mṛṇan pramṛṇan* ।। *mroko manohā khano nirdāha ātmadūṣistanūdūṣiḥ* ।।
>
> The rain is falling heavily as the bullock free from the staff. The lightning fire is also vigorously damaging all that is coming in its way. Violently slaying the people, as if slaying their minds, dashing down everything as it wishes, the fire is burning the lives and livestocks of all.[9]

The noise-pollution is also taken into consideration by the *AV* as in the following song:

> *ālāpāśca pralāpāścābhilāpalapāśca ye* ।
> *śarīraṃ sarve prāviśannāyujaḥ prayujo yujaḥ* ।।

> The speeches loud indeed and very loud talk, the sounds nearby and far fastened and entered the bodies as a crowd, gathered, scattered and violently coming together.[10]

The Ātharvaṇa seers, for example, Garutmān, have implied that the insects and serpents, etc. because of the natural hazards introduce their poisons and viruses into the animal bodies. These viruses also originate in some of the five basic elements of nature and enter and infect human beings through mosquitoes, other insects and germs designated as Ṁalimluca, Darṇāma, Baja, etc.

> *yadagnau Sūryé viṣaṃ Pṛthivyāmoṣádhīṣu yat* ।
>
> *kāndāviṣaṃ kanaknákaṃ niraitvaitú te viṣam* ।।
>
> We scare away the poison from you which is (infected) by Agni — the fire, Sūrya — the sun (through the stroke) and which is generated in the Earth and Plants.[11]

All these have resulted in physical destruction of the human life, causing diseases. A list of the diseases/defects/afflictions and their references in the *AV* follows:

Leprosy : 1.23, 1.24, 5.4, 6.95, 19.39.
Pains in joints : 2.9.
Tuberculosis : 2.33, 6.14, 6.20, 6.85, 6.127, 9.8, 12.2, 19.38.
Eye defects : 4.20.
Urine defects : 1.3.
Defect in embryo : 8.6.
Cough : 6.105.
Rheumatic-afflictions : 4.12, 6.109.
Pain in teeth : 6.140.
Pain in arms and legs : 1.18.
Tonsils : 6.83, 7.74, 7.76.
Fever : 1.25, 5.22, 7.116.
Poisoning : 4.6, 4.7, 5.13, 6.12, 6.100, 7.56, 7.88, 10.4.
Haemorrhage : 1.17, 6.44.
Jaundice : 1.22.

Asthma : 1.12
Aids : 2.8, 3.7.

PROTECTION FROM HAZARDS

The *AV-saṁhitā* has, generally speaking, preserved in its contents some very useful remedies for natural calamities. These remedies may be useful against natural hazards even in the present day. The text of the *AV* advises that the five elements — fire, water, air, earth and wind — be maintained pure. We should not allow impurities in water under common use to enter the drain on occasions such as marriage. We should always treat the components of nature very politely. It is desired that the elements of nature remain standstill everywhere in the universe:

> *asthā̱d Daurasthā́d Pṛthi̱vyasthā̱d viśvā́mi̱daṃ jagā́t* ।
> *ā̱sthāne̱ parvátā asyu̱ stāmnyasvā́ṅ atiṣṭ̱hipaṃ* ।।
>
> The sky would remain standstill, standstill would be the Earth, all this world would be erect and conformed. The hilly regions would be standstill and the horses would be standstill in their shelter.[12]

The sunlight is very much invoked in *AV* verses to cover the villages and remove impurities from the atmosphere. The *Jālāṣa Karma*, the process of collecting the water in lakes and tanks from time to time for preserving it, is very often criticized in the *AV-saṁhitā*. Great hospitality has been offered to the plants and forests in the *AV* and every now and then, there are hymns referring to conflagration in nature:

> *śaṃ tápa̱ mātí tapo̱ Agne̱ mā ta̱nvā́ṃ 1 tapā́ḥ* ।
> *vanéṣu śuṣmó astu te Pṛthi̱vyāmástu̱ yaddharā́ḥ* ।।
>
> O Firegod, enlight with heat that is bearable and not unbearable. Please do not heat our bodies and you would be prosperous towards that you take with you from forests and the Earth.[13]

However, some common practices were introduced by the *AV* seers to offer protection from insects and germs — for example, smoke, heat and light produced in spells involving the use of Ajaśṛṅgī safeguarded human beings from infection by evil bodies. Everyone should be confident about the treatment extended by the physician. A person, in general, should keep himself away from infection of any kind but, if injured, should try to remove the root-cause of the injury from the body as directed by the medical practitioner. Everyone should bear in mind the seven prohibitions advised by the *AV* seers to overcome any evil effects, physical or mental:

> *saptamaryādā́ḥ kavayástatakṣustāsāmidekā́mabhyaṃ'huro gā́t* ।
> *āyorhá skambha upámasya nīḍe pathāṃ visárge dharuṇéṣu tasthau* ।।

> O Skumbha, the lifegod, the scholars have laid down seven limitations to the mischievous deeds of the people, out of which even if a single one is crossed, the Ahura — the Varuṇa — would assign him (in the religious way) to the extremity of this world.[14]

The Cultural Environment

It is true that culture creates humanity in human beings. Culture develops the mind, intellect and self-respect of the human being. The great *Saṁhitā* of *AV*, in its songs, aimed to secure harmony in the society, the *Sāṃmanasyāni-sūktāni*, the all-pervading good character of the human mind at its time. The culture of the Indian society signalizing this unity of its members is referred to with great respect in the following verse:

> *sahṛdayaṃ sāṃmanasyamavídveṣaṃ kṛṇomi vaḥ* ।
> *anyo anyamabhi háryata vatsaṃ jātamivā́ghnyā* ।।

> I am to procure for you the kindness and harmony of your mind and one would take another hand in hand for better

prospects as the cow (non-slaughterable) accompanies her newly-born calf.[15]

A unique character of the Indian society that originated in its long Vedic period is that it always seems ready to accept even its foemen for merging in it. All the thoughts in the *AV* hymns on nationality, unity and liberality invoke the cultural environment in which the people of its time were living, for example:

saṃ vo̱ manā́ṃsi̱ saṃ vra̱tā samākū́tīrnamāmasi |

a̱mī ye vivrátā̱ sthana̱ tānva̱h saṃ námayāmasi ||

We salute the unity of our mind, unity in our undertakings and pay reverence to the unity of our heart. We cooperate with them also who are apart or rather adverse towards our ways of life.[16]

Owing to this peculiarity of the *AV*, it might have been accepted later on by the Vedic tradition and exhalted as the text-book of the Brahmā priest, the head of the office of ritual. The great poet of India, Kālidāsa, therefore, designates the priest Vasiṣṭha as 'Ātharvaṇo Jñānanidhiḥ' in his famous epic, *Raghuvaṃśam*.

CULTURAL POLLUTION AND THE REMEDY

What happened later to the commons, especially the farmers and their village-families, to make them illiterate and how did they become victims of oppression by the wild curses of their foemen and why half of the Indian population, the women, achieved subsidiary status every now and then? Certainly cultural pollution resulted in this misfortune of the masses and it might have continued at double speed as time advanced through one generation after another!

Āryans and other invaders arrived in India, conquered it and ruled over the masses. The winners established their colonies of warriors and religious priests, keeping the masses away from the throne as well as from the office of ritual that belonged to them. In the very first conquest of the Āryan invaders, they drove away the literature and culture of the Indian aboriginals. This common cult of aboriginals in India of the *AV* time was seriously influenced by the Āryan culture. The people, denied education, underwent hybridization of culture and started practising various magical rites and incantations through spells and sorceries belonging to their own faculty of impressions. Unfortunately, all this resulted in various blind faiths and created various real and imaginary calamities in their lives. These are listed below along with their references in the *AV* text:

Wickedness : 1.10, 3.31, 4.23-28, 33, 6.26, 112, 114, 115, 7.34, 64, 112, 115, 8.1, 2, 11.6.
Curse : 2.7, 6.37, 7.59
Purity-Impurity : 2.23.
Miserliness : 6.71.
Lustfulness : 3.21, 25, 6.130, 131, 132, 9.2, 19.52.
Obstructing : 6.63, 112, 121, 7.77, 7.78, 83.
Amorousness : 1.31, 7.113.
Sorrow : 6.93, 16.3.
Bad dreams : 6.45, 46, 7.23, 100, 101, 16.5-9, 19.56, 57.
Incantations : 2.11, 5.14, 31, 10.1.
Evil-emulation : 1.28, 7.108, 114, 8.3, 6.18, 7.45.

Even though thousands of years have passed we still see similarities between the masses in the period of the *AV* as depicted in that *Veda* and the masses of the present time. This land originally belonging to the hard-working agrarians is very easy to rule; this can be straightway impressed by any hypothesis regarding any faculty of impressions. The common farmer of this country, accepting all possible changes in his tools and instruments, fertilizers and, moreover, insecticides irrespective of this country's environmental distinction from other countries, practises only agriculture on a large scale even at the sunset of the twentieth century. And because of his paying hardware duty ignorantly, he is always encountering violence of his achievements even at the end of fifty years of his independence!

Governing bodies in religion and politics are rather very much against him. These do not excuse him from any payment of taxes or fee for religious rituals performed. Therefore, he should keep out the influence of religion and politics on him and try to come out of the muddy meadows of ruddy customs of various kinds. Otherwise, these will always oppress him and keep him in fright with sorrow, poverty and illiteracy resulting as the achievements from these. No politician from any class or belonging to any political party will recognize him and pay any reverence to his hard work. So he must again meet his true assistants from his village community and with their advanced knowledge in village occupations try to revive his ancient scholarship.

The farmer should build up his own career and character and that of his family-members of his native place. They should create opportunities within the field of agriculture for their scholar-agriculturists, scholar-traders, commercial agents, bankers and scholar-workmen. It is to the pride of the hardworking community in India that the treasure of excellent advice and information regarding their skill in occupations lies buried here in the foundation of the ancient Indian Vedic literature, in the *Atharvaveda,* which invokes:

madhúmatīroṣádhīrdyāva Āpo madhúmanno bhavatvanta riksam ।
kṣetrásya patīrmadhúmānno astvariṣyanto anvénaṃ carema ।।

Saturated with nectar the plants and crops would be,
Sky, atmosphere and waters sprinkled with honey would be,
Agrarian ours, the master of farms prosperous with nectar would be.
And uninjured we would be his followers till there he would be![17]

References

1. *Atharvaveda kā Subodha-bhāṣya, bhāga* 1-1.1.1.
2. 1.15.1, 1.1, 3, 12, 13, 15, 2.3, 3.21, 26, 27, 5.9, 10, 24, 6.3, 4, 10, 23, 24, 38, 30, 33.
3. 8.7.1.
4. 8.7.3.
5. 6.38.1.
6. 8.6, 5, 11.8, 8.6, 10.4, 5, 10, 15.6, 7.
7. 11.4.26.
8. 6.40, 52, 53, 55, 57, 62, 77, 80, 88, 91, 93, 100, 120, 124, 128, 129, 7.6, 11, 13, 14, 18, 39, 66, 69, 89, 97, 12.1, 3.
9. 16.1.1 to 3.
10. 11.8.25.
11. 10.4.22.
12. 6.77.1.
13. 18.2.36.
14. 5.1.6.
15. 3.30.1.
16. 3.8.5.
17. 20.143.8.

Appendices

Appendix 1 : Vedic Mantras in Sanskrit Literature

1	2	3	4	5	6	7
Sr. No.	*Name of the book*	*Trayi*	*Ṛk-Yajus*	*Yajus-Sāma*	*Ṛk-Sāma*	*Ṛk only*
1.	*Ṛgveda Saṃhitā*	*Maṇḍala*-10 *Sūkta*-90 *Ṛk*-9	—	—	5.44.14,15, 10.36.5, 10.85.11, 10.114.6	1.164.39, 2.3.7, 2.35.12, 3.2.4, 5.6.5, 5.28.4, 5.64.1-4, 6.8.4, 8.16.47, 8.23. 3, 8.27.1-5, 9.68.1, 9.74.3, 10.64.4, 10.71. 11, 10.77.7, 10.91.12, 10. 105.8, 10.113. 3, 10.165.5.
2.	*Aitareya Brāhmaṇa*	*Pañcikā*-1 *Adhyāya*-3 *Brāhmaṇa*-22 5.5.32, 33, 8.3.12, 8.4.17, 19.	8.4.18	—	2.3.23, 24, 3.2.23, 8.1.2, 8.3.13, 14, 8.5.27.	1.1.3, 1.3.13, 14, 16, 17, 1.4.25, 1.5.28-30, 2.1.2, 5, 2.2. 16, 18, 3.1.3, 4, 7, 8, 11, 3.3.38, 3.4.43, 3.5.47, 50, 4.1.1, 4.2.7, 4.3.21, 4.4.25, 5.1.4, 5.3.17, 6.1.1, 2, 6.2.7, 6.4.20, 24, 6.5. 32-34, 7.2.5, 7.3.16, 18, 8.1.3, 9.
3.	*Aitareya Āraṇyaka*	*Āraṇyaka*-1, *Adhyāya*-3, *Khaṇḍa*-3, 2.3.6, 3.2.3, 5.	—	—	—	1.1.1., 1.3.8, 2.2.2, 2.3.6, 3.2.5, 6, 5.1.1, 5.2.1, 4, 5, 5, 3.1.
4.	*Śāṅkhāyana Āraṇyaka*	*Adhyāya*-1 *Khaṇḍa*-1 3.5., 3.7, 4.6, 8.3, 8.8.	—	—	3.5, 7.14	1.2, 2.1, 2.2, 2.3, 2.5, 6, 10, 11, 16, 4.8, 8.5, 11.

— The Old Age (2500-0 BC Approximately)

8	9	10	11	12
Yajus only	*Sāma only*	*Uktha, Brahma, Gāthā etc.*	*Atharvan, Bhṛgu, Aṅgiras*	*Atharvavedic Verse*
7.41.8, 10.12.3, 10.106.3.	1.173.1, 2.23.17, 2.43.1, 2, 5.54. 14, 7.33.14, 8.16. 9, 8.29.10, 8.66. 9, 10.78.5, 10.99. 2, 10.107.6.	7.26.2, 7.28.1, 2, 5, 7.29.2-5, 7.30.5, 7. 31.2, 11, 7.32.2, 7. 34.16, 7.69.2, 8.71. 14, 9.99.4, 10.54.6, 10.56.7, 10.65.14.	1.1.6, 31.1, 2, 17, 45.3, 51.3, 62.1, 2, 3, 71.4, 80.16, 83.4, 5, 102.1, 107.2, 121.1, 3, 4.6.11, 6.15.17, 7.42.1, 9.11.2, 10.14.6, 10.108. 8, 10.	—
1.2.8, 1.5.29, 30, 5.5.28, 7. 4.21, 22, 24.	2.5.37, 3.1.4, 4.1. 2, 4.2.13, 4.3.19, 4.5.21, 31, 5.1.1, 4, 5.2.1, 7, 12, 5. 3.16, 18, 5.4.20, 25, 8.1.1.	2.5.35, 37, 38, 40, 3.1.1, 11, 3.2.12, 19, 3.4.41, 42, 43, 3.5.43, 49, 4.1.3, 6.5.32, 7.5.34, 8.4. 21.	4.3.17, 5.1.2, 5.2. 14, 5.4.20, 6.2.7, 6.5.34, 35, 8.3.12, 14, 8.4.21.	—
—	2.3.4, 3.1.5, 5.1. 5, 5.1.6, 5.2.5.	1.1.3, 1.2.1, 2, 4, 1.3.7, 8, 1.5.2, 2.1.2, 5.1.6, 5.3.2	—	—
—	1.4, 2.1, 10, 3.5.	1.2, 1.4, 1.8., 2.1, 2.18, 5.3	1.4, 2.17, 12.4-8 (*Irāmaṇi, Bailva, Pratisara*)	14.1.
	—	—	—	2.6.

1	2	3	4	5	6	7
5.	*Kauṣītaki Brāhmaṇopaniṣada*	*Adhyāya*-1 *Mantra*-5, 1.6, 2.4.	—	—	—	—
6.	*Āśvalāyana Śrauta Sūtra*	—	*Pūrvaṣaṭka-Adhyāya* 2-*Kāṇḍikā* 13	—	*Pūrvaṣaṭka* 5.12, *Uttaraṣaṭka*-3.10	*Pūrvaṣaṭka*-1.2, 2.12, 16, 17, 3.1, 2, 6, 8, 4.2, 4, 5 9, 15, 5.7, 9, 10, 14, 18, 6.2, 4, 6. *Uttaraṣaṭka*-1.1, 5, 11, 2.1, 2, 12, 3.5.
7.	*Āśvalāyana Gṛhya-Sūtra*	—	—	—	*Adhyāya*-1 *Kāṇḍikā* 7, 3.10	1.1, 8, 12, 20, 23, 2.1, 9, 3.7, 9, 4.6, 7.
8.	*Sāmaveda Kauthuma*	—	—	—	*Aindra Kāṇḍa*-4.4.8.10	*Uttarārcika*—6. 3.7.2
9.	*Sāmavedīya Jaiminīya Brāhmaṇa.*	*Kāṇḍa*-1 *Khaṇḍa*-2 *Brāhmaṇa*-2	2.23.3	1.225.1	1.76.1, 127.1, 2 128.2 to 3	1.52.1, 2, 81.5, 96.3, 100.1, 104.6, 112.1, 119.1-3, 121.1, 139.3 to 3.12.1, 306.1
10.	*Sāmavedīya Taṇḍya Mahābrāhmaṇa.*	—	—	—	*Adhyāya*-4. *Khaṇḍa*-3. *Stotra*-4, 5, 6, 7.7.1, 2, 8.1.7, 12.6 8, 13.12.13, 15.5.26.	2.2.2, 4.9.4, 5.6.6, 8.8.24, 9.3.6, 9.8.7, 9, 10.9.1, 11.1.6, 13.1.9-12, 13.7.11, 14.1.7, 15.1.9-11, 23.16. 6.

8	9	10	11	12
—	*Pūrvaṣaṭka*-1.3, 5, 4.12, 5.15, 6. 5, 8, 10, 13, *Uttaraṣaṭka*-1. 5, 8, 2.4, 5, 6, 12, 3.3, 6, 8, 5.3, 6.7.	*Pūrvaṣaṭka*-1.3, 5, 8, 2.7, 12, 4.12, 13, 5.5, 8, 13, 6.12.	*Pūrvaṣaṭka*-2.3, 5, 7, 8, 10, 3.8, 10, 4.1, 3, 13, 5.20, 6.3, *Uttaraṣaṭka*-1.7, 2.1, 11, 4.2, 6.2, 5, 10, 11, 16.	*Pūrva-ṣaṭka*-3.5, 6. *Uttara-ṣaṭka*-3. 14, 4.7.
Pūrvaṣaṭka-3.2, 6.12.	1.21	1.3	—	3.3, 4.7.
—	*Aindrakāṇḍa*-4.4.10.8.	—	*Uttarārcika*-1.1.1.2 *Āgneyakāṇḍa*-1.1.2.8. *Pavamāna Soma Kāṇḍa*-5.6.3.9.	—
Araṇyakāṇḍa 6.1.7. *Yājiṣṭha Yajmahe, Yajyave.* 1.58.1, 353.4, 2.206.1.	1.68.1, 2, 69.1, 2, 70.1, 71.3, 91.1, 111.1, 112.3, 4, 117.1, 4, 122.1-4, 123.2, 3, 124.3, 127.5, 137.1, 140. 1, 144.2, 3, 147.1, 148.1, 2, 150.1, 151.1, 155.1, 157. 2, 158.1, 160.1, 5, 163.4, 164.1, 2, 165.4, 166.2, in all *Khaṇḍas*	1.4.1, 5.1, 37.1, 4, 94.1, 179.1, 201.4, 202.1, 2, 206.3, 207.1, 2, 212.2, 274.2, 276.3, 277.1, 278.1, 279.2, 286.1, 2.7.2, 24.1, 50.2, 84.3, 108.6, 131.1, 3.41. 1, etc.	1.31.1, 42.1, 81. 4, 168.1, 183.1, 224.2, 2.14.1, 116.1, 117.1, 120.1, 121.1, 122.1, 235.1, 290.1, 362, 365, 366, 402.1, 3.28. 1, 32.1, 43.1, 47.1, 51.1, 53.1, 56.1, 63.1, 64.1, 77.1, 160.1, 188. 1, 209.1, 223.1, 270.1, 312.1, 368.1, 381.1, 382.1, etc.	—
1.6.4, 1.6.9.	4.2.19, 3.1, 2, 7, 8, 9, 5.1, 6.12, 8.10, 5.2.5, 10, 12, 3.1, 2, 6, 7, 6.4.8, 9, 13, 6.18, 7.3.2, 4, 6, 16, 7. 6.17, 8.1.6, 8, 9,	2.16.4, 4.5.19, 8.8. 1, 2, 5, 8, 25, 10.3, 9.1.1, 25-27, 4.15, 7.11, 10.4.5, 11.4. 6, 10.17, 11.2, 12. 3.8, 16, 13.5.8, 19, 16.10.1, 18.5.24,	1.8.11, 8.2.5, 6, 8.22, 9.4, 5, 11.8. 8, 10, 11.10.9, 12.3.22, 23, 5.11, 6.12, 8.6, 9.8, 10, 13.3.24, 9.24, 11.10, 14, 22,	—

1	2	3	4	5	6	7
11.	*Jaiminiya Upaniṣad Brāhmaṇa (Āraṇyaka).*	*Adhyāya*-1. *Anuvāka*-1. *Khaṇḍa*-1. *Kāṇḍikā*-1-5. 1.2.1.1, 3, 5, 10, 1.3.3.3, 1.4.4.10, 1.5.1.2, 1.14.4.3, 1.17.2.2, 1.18.2.3, 7, 1.18.3.2, 2.3. 3.7, 3.4.1.7-9, 3.4.3.1, 3.4.4.4, 4.11.3.12.	—	—	1.2.2.2, 1.4. 1.3, 1.4.2.4, 10, 12, 1.4.3. 1, 1.18.1.1, 10, 1.18.2.2, 2.1.2.9, 10, 3.7.1.10, 4.11.2.1.	1.4.1.6, 1.4.2.5, 4.11.2.4.
12.	*Upaniṣads* on *Sāmaveda*	*Chāndogya* — *Adhyāya*-1, *Khaṇḍa*-1, *Mantra*-2, 3.15.7, 4. 17.2, 6.7.2 *Yogacūḍāmaṇi-Khaṇḍa*-74, *Avyaktopaniṣada-Khaṇḍa*-3, 5, *Jābālyupaniṣada*				
13.	*Sāmavediya Drāhyāyaṇa-Śrauta Sūtra*	*Paṭala*-10. *Khaṇḍa*-4. *Sūtra*-8.	—	—	3.3.19, 8.1.8, 8.2.25, 18.1. 14.	1.1.6, 2.1.2, 2.2. 13, 3.1.16, 3.2. 19, 6.1.13, 7.1. 27, 8.2.5, 8.3.11, 9.1.4, 9.3.11, 11. 3.4, 12.1.32, 16. 1.5, 20.3.20, 21. 3.2.

8	9	10	11	12
	12, 2.1, 3, 8.5.14, 8.11, 26, 10.3, 9. 1.33, 2.19, 22, 23, 4.10, 5.8, 6.1, 2, 8, 9, 9.13, 10. 4.7, 6.3, 4, 6, 13. 3.19, 4.18, 6.9, 9.17, 22, 12.5, 14.3.10, 13, 4.7, 5.15, 18.5.17, 18, 21.2.3, 23.3.9.	6.1.	14.3.22, 25, 9.9, 32, 15.9.9, 16. 10.9, 10, 14.2, 18.9.1, 20.11.3, 4, 25.2.1, 2, 16.2.	
1.8.1.9, 1.8.2.3, 7.	1.1.1.8, 1.1.3.7, 1.1.4.6, 1.1.6.1, 6, 1.3.1.3, 1.3. 2.5, 1.3.3.7, 1. 3.4.2, 3, 1.4.2. 6-8, 1.5.1.1, 3, 1.6.1.6, 1.18.4. 3, 14, 2.5.3.4-6, 3.1.1.12, 18, 19, 3.2.1.1, 4-7, 3.2.4.10, 4.8.3.2, 4.11.2.3.	1.2.2.4, 1.16.1.4, 1.17.1.9, 1.18.2.1, 3.4.1.1, 2.	2.4.2.9, 3.5.2.3.	—
				3.1.2, 7.1. 2, *Maitrāyaṇī Prapāṭhaka*-6, *Khaṇḍa*-32, 33, *Mahopaniṣada-Adhyāya*-1.
1.1.5, 2.4.5, 3.1.4, 7.1.28, 12.1.24, 26, 13.1.1, 14.3.2, 15.1.2.	2.1.1, 2.1.11, 2. 2.16, 2.4.7, 3. 4.2, 6.2.2, 6.3.1, 7.1.19, 8.1.6, 9. 1.15, 9.3.4, 11. 2.5, 12.2.14, 13.4.15, 16.1.6, 18.2.1, 21.4.10.	—	18.2.18, 18.3.16, 18.4.6, 21, 19.1. 2, 19.2.1, 19.3. 1, 14.4.15, 20. 1.26, 20.2.34, 20.3.5, 32, 21. 3.19.	*As Ātharvaṇa Verse-Yosmāndveṣṭi*-4. 2.2, 13.3. 22, *Dundubhi*-10. 3.4, *Śaṃnodevīḥ* 13.3.11.

1	2	3	4	5	6	7
14.	*Sāma-vedīya Khādira Gṛhya Sūtra*	—	—	—	*Paṭala*-2. *Khaṇḍa*-5. *Sūtra*-34.	*Tṛc* — 1.2.6.
15.	*Śukla Yajur-veda Vāja-saneyi Mādh-yandina Saṁ-hitā*	*Adhyāya*-4. *Kāṇḍikā*-1. 18.29, 67, 20.12, 31.7, 36.1	—	12.4, 19.28	4.9, 18.43	11.8, 19.25
16.	*Śukla Yajur-vedīya Mādh-yandina Śākhīya Śata-patha Brāh-maṇa*	*Kāṇḍa*-1 *Prapāṭhaka*-1 *Brāhmaṇa*-4 *Mantra*-2. 2.1.4.6, 10, 2.5.5.2, 3.1.1.12, 3.1.5.37 4.2.2.7, 4.3.1.5, 4.3.3.11, 13, 4.5. 4.1, 9.1, 5, 19, 11.20, 5.1.1.10, 5.4.7.1, 6.1.1.8, 10, 6.2.3.10, 11, 20, 6.4. 1.4.	1.1.4.9 1.6.2.20 1.7.2.3 1.7.4.8 3.1.5.38 7.4.1.4.	5.1. 5.17, 6.5. 2.6	2.4.3.46, 3.1.5.5, 4.3.5.6, 4.5.9.11-13, 6.5.1.7.	1.5.2.27, 29, 40, 2.1.4.5, 29, 30, 2.4.2.2, 3.5.3.1, 3.6.4.31, 3.7.5.25 4.2.6.3, 4.3.1.8, 5.4.6.28, 7.4, 7.2. 2.15, 16, 21, 22, 7.2.3.43, 7.4.2.25, 26.
17.	*Bṛhat-Āraṇyaka Upani-ṣad*	*Adhyāya*-1, *Brāh-maṇa*-5, *Khaṇḍa*-5, 5.15.2, 1.2.5.	—	—	—	—

8	9	10	11	12
2.1.9.	—	—	—	—
—	—	—	4.10, 8.56, 11.10, 11, 16, 33, 59, 61, 65, 12.8, 14.6, 15.28, 57, 58, 19.50, 34.12, 16, 38.9.	—
1.1.2.7, 5.7, 22, 6.1, 1.2.2.20, 4. 3, 5.18, 1.7.3. 23, 2.3.1.17, 3.1.1.4, 11, 4. 1, 14, 16, 3.2. 6.16, 3.3.2.7, 3.4.2.11, 4.4, 5.4, 17, 3.5.4.8, 3.6.3.13, 4.32, 3.7.3.17, 4.1.2. 21, 4.3.5.11, 6.1, 4.4.3.4, 10, 5.1.5.7, 10, 15, 6.1.2.31, 6.2.3. 43, 4.8, 6.3.3.4, 4.10, 5.2, 5, 7. 6, 6.4.1.6, 7, 11, 2.10, 11, 4.5, 6, 6.5.3.8, 5.1, 7, 7.1.2.16, 17, 20, 7.1.3.20, 4.1, 10, 13, 19, 7.2.2. 29, 30, 3.21-25-31-40-44, 7.3. 2.5-14-20-24-36-39, 7.4.1.29.	1.6.3.19, 2.2.2. 12, 3.3.3.16, 4. 4.1.6, 4.5.11.11, 12, 5.1.5.1, 5.3. 3.3, 7.2.4.17, 7. 3.1.3.	—	1.1.5.13, 1.2.3. 26, 1.3.6.25, 3.1. 5.10, 14, 3.4.1. 13, 19, 32, 4.1.5. 1, 4.4.1.20, 2.8, 6.1.2.28, 6.2.3. 38, 39, 6.2.4.9, 6.3.1.4, 6.3.2.1, 6.3.3.2, 3, 6.3. 5.4, 14, 7.2-6, 6. 4.1.10, 6.4.2.3-6, 8, 17, 6.5.3.6, 7.1.1.30.	—
—	—	—	—	2.4.10, 4. 6.11, 4.1. 2.

1	2	3	4	5	6	7
18.	*Upaniṣads* on *Śukla Yajurveda*	*Subālopaniṣada Khaṇḍa*-6	—	—	—	—
19.	*Kātyāyana Śrauta Sūtra*	*Adhyāya*-1. *Kāṇḍikā*-3. *Sūtra*-1, 25.8.6, 25.1.8, 25.14.36, 37	18.6. 20.	24.7. 20.	7.3.20.	4.8.3, 14.4.3, 5, 15.6.3, 16.1.38, 2.9, 4.40, 17.2.1, 12, 18.2.11, 18.3. 17, 19.1.11, 4.12, 20.8.6, 21.1.6, 25.1.10, 10.13, 11.34, 14.19.
20.	*Pāraskara Gṛhyasūtra.*	—	*Pariśiṣṭa Śrāddha Sūtra*-3	—	—	*Kāṇḍa*-1; *Kāṇḍikā*-3. *Sūtra*-21, 1.16.9, 2.3.5, 6.13, 11.12.
21.	*Kṛṣṇa Yajurveda Taittirīya saṃhitā*	*Kāṇḍa*-1. *Prapāṭhaka* 2. *Anuvāka*-3, 2.4.12, 2.5.7, 3.1.1,4.7.9, 6.5.10, 7.3.1, 12.	6.1.9, 11, 6.3. 2, 6.5. 11, 6. 6.2.	—	1.2.2, 3.4.7, 5.4.8, 6.1.3, 6.5.9, 7.5.1.	6.1.2, 6.3.11, 6.5. 6, 6.6.7.
22.	*Kṛṣṇa Yajurvedīya Taittirīya Brāhmaṇa*	*Kāṇḍa*-1, *Prapāṭhaka*-2, *Anuvāka*-1, *Mantra*-26, 2.6. 5.8.	2.1.9. 1, 2.	2.3. 2.4.	1.4.4.9, 1.6.3.9.	1.3.1.
23.	*Kṛṣṇa Yajurvedīyam Taittirīya Āraṇyakam*	*Adhyāya*-1, *Prapāṭhaka*-3, *Anuvāka*-3, *Khaṇḍa*-12, 1.7.7.5, 1.10. 10.13, 63.	—	—	—	1.2.11, 10.40, 66.

8	9	10	11	12
—	—	—	—	*Muktiko-panisad Adhyaya*-1.11-13.
7.2.27, 28, 8.3.13, 10.8.13, 11.1.6, 14.3.18, 4.12, 17.3.24, 4.20, 22.6.11, 25.1.14, 10.16.	10.8.18, 13.2.7, 14.4.1, 17.3.27, 4.4, 18.3.1, 16, 19.5.1, 24.1.18 2.6, 6.40, 25.12.15, 26.2.11, 7.6, 27.	—	15.4.1, 23.2.3, 23.5.22, 24.3.1, 24.4.11.	As Atharvavedic Verse-3.3.2. *Samiti*-3.5.4. *Bhaiṣajya*-15.7.32, *Maṇi*, 25.7.17.
Pariśiṣṭa Bhojana Sūtra-1.	1.5.9, 3.14.2-5, *Akṣayya-tṛpti Prakaraṇa-Kāṇḍikā*-8	1.7.2, 1.15.9	2.10.4-6, *Pariśiṣṭa Śauca*-Page-410, 1.3.8, 1.4.1, 2.13.3, 4, 2.14.5-26, 3.1.4, 3.15.20.	—
1.1.10, 10, 1.5.2, 16.9, 6.1.7, 10, 6.2.2, 10, 6.4.3, 4, 6.6.3.	1.6.10, 1.6.12, 4.4.2, 4.4.12, 7.1.1, 4, 7.5.9.	7.5.11.	1.1.7, 1.2.12, 1.3.14, 2.6.12, 3.5.11, 4.1.3, 5, 6, 4.2.1, 4.3.6, 4.4.3, 4, 6, 5.1.4, 5, 5.2.8, 4.3, 5.6.6, 7.2, 6.1.1, 3, 2.7, 7.1.18, 4.17.	Agriculture-4.2.5-10, 5.2.5, 7.5.11
1.3.5, 1.4.3.2, 1.6.5.5, 1.7.10.2, 2.1.2.8, 2.1.4.6, 2.2.4.2, 2.4.2.1.	1.2.3, 1.3.6.2, 1.4.5.2, 1.4.6.3, 7.7, 1.8.2.5, 2.2.9.7, 2.6.5.2.	—	1.1.4.8, 10.4, 1.2.1.10, 25, 1.3.6.1, 1.8.2.1, 1.8.6.2.1.1.1, 2.2.3.6, 2.2.5.3, 7.7, 10.5, 11.5, 2.3.2.5, 4.6, 2.6.2.2.	—
1.2.11, 3.8, 4.2, 3, 4-11, 5.2, 3, 4, 6, 7, 8, 10, 6.1, 12, 10.12.	1.2.17, 3.1, 4.1, 11, 5.9, 10, 7.2, 9.1, 5.	1.7.7.5, 1.3.8, 4.7, 5.6.	1.1.10.7, 1.2.10.1, 1.3.8, 10, 4.9, 39, 5.7.	*Yosmān-dveṣṭi*-1.2.5, 1.2.9.1, 1.4.4.10, 11, 23, 42, *Bheṣaja*-4.42,

1	2	3	4	5	6	7
24.	*Kṛṣṇa Yajur-vedīya Upani-ṣads.*	*Taittirīya-Śikṣā-dhyāya-Anuvāka-*5.2, *Kālāgni-rudra, Dhyāna-bindu Ślokas*-9-11, *Brahmavidyā*-4-6, *Ekākṣara*-7.				
25.	*Bhāra-dvāja Śrauta Sūtram*	—	*Praśna*-4. *Kāṇ-ḍikā*-17. *Sūtra*-3, 13. 16.13.	—	9.3.1, 13.1, 10.5.15	5.8.6, 6.3.11, 13, 7.20.5, 9.3.2, 8.3, 10.22.4, 11.18.9, 10, 13.9.3, 28.4, 14.14.11.
26.	*Bhāra-dvāja Gṛhya-sūtra.*	*Praśna*-2. *Khaṇḍa*-14, 2. 24.	—	—	—	1.9, 2.28.
27.	*Āpas-tambīya Gṛhya-sūtra*	—	—	—	—	*Paṭala*-4, *Khaṇḍa*-11. *Sūtra*-10, 12, 5. 12.13.
28.	*Vārāha GṛS.*	*Khaṇḍa*-6, 8.	—	—	—	1, 14.

8	9	10	11	12
				Yosmān-dveṣṭi- 1.5.5.9, 10, 1.7.8. 3, 1.10. 10.1.
—	—	—	—	*Taittirīya* 2.3, 2.10, *Rudrahṛ-daya Ślokas* 28, 29.
1.21.5, 24.11, 25.3, 2.1.4, 5, 6.10, 3.12.1, 4.6.5, 19.8, 9, 5.14.12, 7.17.8 22.16, 17, 8.4. 9, 10, 5.10, 11. 5, 21.15, 24.11, 9.1.15, 10.7.4, 16.10, 18.10, 22.8, 11.1.2, 12.2.14, 13.5. 10, 14.17.10, 19.9, 10. *Pitṛmedhika* etc.	5.10.6, 7, 17.9, 18.1, 8.11.8, 11. 13.13, 14.14.1, 2, 20.7, 13.14.1, 2, 14.21.5, 6.		[1.12.13, 24.1, 4. 12.4, 9.16.8, 18. 7, 4.18.7, 5.11.7.]	*Śaṃno-devīḥ Abhīṣṭa-ye*, 5.4.13.
3.12.	3.1.	2.21.	3.9.	3.11, 3.14.
2.4.5, 8, 2.6.11, 4.10.5, 12, 4. 11.7, 5.12.3, 5.	—	—	—	—
—	—	—	4.	—

1	2	3	4	5	6	7
29.	*Bodhāyana Gṛhya-Sūtra.*	*Praśna*-1, *Adhyāya*-2, *Sūtra*-34, 3.3.34, 4.5.4, *Paribhāṣā*-1.1.19, 1.4.17.	—	—	—	2.1.7, 17, 2.5.40, *Gṛhyaśeṣa* 1.1. 24, 14.7, 8, 15.6, 16.25, 2.7.6, 2.16. 17, 3.12.1, 20.3, 21.3, 4.5.11, 5.6. 8, 8.2, *Pitṛmedha* 1.8.10, 2.5.6, 7, 7.3.
30.	*Atharvavedīya Śaunakīya Saṁhitā*	*Kāṇḍa*-7. *Sūkta*-54. Verse-2.	—	—	—	—
31.	*Gopatha Brāhmaṇa*	*Pūrvabhāga*-1. *Prapāṭhaka-1.* *Kāṇḍikā*-6, 23, 24, 28, 31, 3.1, 5.25.	*Uttarabhāga* 2.4.2.	—	*Uttarabhāga*-2.3.9, 20.	1.1.9, 12, 22, 2.1, 7, 8, 15, *Ṛgveda*-1.1.7, 5.16, 1.2. 17, 20, 21, 23, 3. 20, 4.17, 23, 5.5, 2.2.4, 14, 24. *Uttarabhāga*-2.3.3, 4, 23, 4.6, 15, 16, 5.10, 13, 6.2, 5, 6.8, 10, 12.
32.	*Atharvavedīya Upaniṣads*	*Praśnopaniṣada-Praśna*-2. *Mantra*-6, 5.7, *Muṇḍakopaniṣada-Muṇḍaka*-2. *Khaṇḍa*-1, *Mantra*-6, 1.1.5, *AtharvaśiraUpaniṣada*-1, *Bṛhajjābāla Upa-niṣada-Brāhmaṇa*-8, *Khaṇḍa*-5, *Nṛsiṃhapūrvatāpanīyopaniṣada-Upaniṣada*-1, *Khaṇḍa*-2, 1.7, 4.2, *Mahānārāyaṇīya Upaniṣada-Khaṇḍa*-22.1, *Sitopaniṣada*-	—	—	—	—

8	9	10	11	12
3.1.22, *Pitṛmedha*-3.4.2, 3.5.6, *Paribhāṣā*-1.3.10, *Gṛhyaśeṣa*-2.17.2, 4.7.2.	—	1.11.11.	1.3.16, 17, 2.2.10, 3.9.3, 3.4.6, 12, *Paribhāṣā*-1.10.18, 17.35-38, 2.5.17. *Gṛhyaśeṣa*-2.15.19, 4.2.22.	1.11.12, 2.9.5, 3.1.8, 2.9, 22, 34, 47, 3.11, 5.7, 9.5, *Gṛhyaśeṣa*-2.7.8, 3.16.8.
—	—	—	—	10.7.20.
Yajurveda-1.1.7, 3.15, 5.17, 2.2.3, 11, 14.	*Sāmaveda*-1.1.19, 5.18, 2.2.14, *Uttarabhāga*-2.5.3, 7, 8, 6.11	—	1.1.5, 7, 13, 3.19, 4.23, 2.1.1, 2.14, 15, 19, 3.17, 4.9, 5.13	1.1.8, 10, 20, 25, 27 29, 2.9, 16, 2.18, 24, 3.1, 2, 3, 16, 4.24, 5.15, 19, 24, 2.2.5, 6, *Uttarabhāga-Yajus avoided*-2.3.9.
—	—	—	—	—

1	2	3	4	5	6	7
		Khaṇḍa-5, *Tripādvibhūtimahānārāyaṇopaniṣada-Adhyāya*-7.				
33.	*Vaitāna Śrautasūtra*	—	—	—	—	*Adhyāya*-3; *Kāṇḍikā*-5; *Sūtra*-16, 8.6, 11.4 *Kha*, 12. 8, 13.14, 4.2.3 *Ka*, 5.1.7, 6.3.18 *Ka*.
34.	*Kauśika Gṛhyasūtra*	*Adhyāya*-, *Kāṇḍikā*-*Sūtra*.	—	—	—	1.4.11, 5.7, 2.16. 29, 5.46.7.
35.	*Pāṇinīya Śikṣā*	*Adhyāya*-10. *Ślokas*-54, 55	—	—	—	—
36.	*Nirukta*	*Adhyāya*-7, *Khaṇḍa*-12, *Pariccheda*-1-4, 13.7.1, 9.1, 10.1, 14.14.	1.16.2	—	—	1.1.1, 2.1.11, 9.1, 17.1, 21.1, 23.1, 3.1.2, 19.9, 6.23.2, 7.9.6, 9.9, 10.1, 20.2, 26.1, 9.7.1, 10.16.2, 21.1, 26. 3, 33.1, 11.12.1, 21.1, 12.2.2, 21. 1, 30.1, 33.1, 40.2, 13.10.1, 11.1, 12. 1, 14.12.
37.	*Pāṇinīya Vyākaraṇa Aṣṭādhyāyī* with *Siddhānta Kaumudī*	*Adhyāya*-2, *Pāda*-4, *Sūtra*-4, 4.2.60.	5.4. 77	—	2.4.14, 5.4.77	4.1.9, 2.4.31, 8.4. 3, 5.4.74, 3.1. 133, 6.3.133, 134, *Phitsūtra*-3.3. 169.
38.	*Gautamapraṇītāni Dharmasūtrāṇi*	*Praśna*-1. *Adhyāya*-1, *Sūtra*-1, *Mitākṣarā*-2.2.3, 25, 2.7.21	—	—	—	3.6.2

8	9	10	11	12
1.2.4, 4.13, 3.6 *Ka*.6, 3.13.19, *Yajurveda*-1.1. 8.	3.10.21 *Kha*, 12. 11, 13.6, 4.3.9, 3. 13, 23, 24, 6.1.9, 8.2.14 *Ka*, *Sāmaveda* 8.4.14 Ka.	4.1.7, 2.4, 3.27, 6.1.20, 6.1.26, 6.3.1 *Ka*.	1.1.5, 2.1.10, 8.3.1 *Ka*.	3.1.2.
2.23.1	1.5.7	—	—	—
—	—	—	—	—
3.19.6, 11.4.1, 31.1, 11.43.1, 12.34.1.	7.4.7, 8.	2.23.1, 4.6.1, 10.12.3, 10.43.1	3.17.1, 5.4.2, 10. 33.1, 11.16.2, 17.1, 19.3, 4, 12.3.3.	1.20.2 (Durgācārya)
Yajvan-8.7.77, 6.1.117-120, 8. 3.104, *Kaskādi Ākṛtigaṇa*-8.6	2.1.43, 5.4.75, 7.1.33, 6.4.170, 135, 4.2.7, 5.2.59, 4.35, 4.125, 1.2. 34, 7.3.1.	4.1.9, 3.129, 3.2.71, *Gaṇapāṭha*, 4.34, 3.2.23.	4.1.101, 102, 107, 108, 6.4.174, 2.4. 65, 5.1.61. *Gaṇapāṭha*-4.2. 38.	4.2.63, 3. 133, 5.1. 124, *Yātū*-4.4.121, *Phitsūtra pāda*-4, *Ākṛti-gaṇa*-5.18, 7.4. *Catur-vedādi-gaṇa*-4.19.
3.2.12	2.6.29	—	*Mitākṣarā* on 1.4.2	*Mitākṣarā* on 1. 3.51, 1.8.5, 3.1.12, 3. 10.47.

1	2	3	4	5	6	7
39.	*Āpastamba Dharma Sūtra.*	*Praśna*-1. *Kāṇḍikā*-2. *Sūtra*-6, 1.12.5, 2.24.8.	—	—	—	1.31.23
40.	*Śrī-Vāsiṣṭha Dharma Śāstram*	*Adhyāya*-1, *Sūtra*-16, 13.33, 17.87	—	—	—	*Ṛgveda*-27.3, 5 28.13.
41.	*Chandaḥ Śāstra*	*Adhyāya*-2. *Sūtra*-6.	—	—	—	2.10
42.	*Vedāṅga Jyotiṣa*	*Vedādi Yajñārthamabhipravṛttāḥ-Adhyāya*-7	—	—	—	—

8	9	10	11	12
—	—	—	—	1.2.2, *Ujjvala* on 1.5.5. 6, 2.29.12.
—	3.19, 23.46, 28.12	—	—	*Cātur-vidya*-3. 20.
2.16	2.9	—	3.66	—
—	—	—	—	—

Appendix 2 : Vedic Mantras in Sanskrit Literature

1	2	3	4	5	6
Sr. No.	*Name of the book*	*Trayī*	*Ṛk only*	*Yajus only*	*Sāma only*
1.	*Manusmṛti*	*Adhyāya*-1. *Śloka*-23. 2.28, 76, 118, 230, 3.1, 4.123, 124, 7.43, 11.261-265, 12.111, 112, 7.37, 8.11, 9.188.	2.77, 80, 181, 3.142, 8.106, 11.249, 252, 254, *Ṛgveda* 11.261.	—	3.185
2.	*Śrī Yājña-valkyasmṛti*	*Adhyāya*-1. *Pra-karṇa*-1, *Śloka*-9, 1. 13.311, 2.15.185, *Traividya*-2.18.211, 3.4.122.	1.10.229, 233, 239	—	1.6.148, 1.10.219, 3.4.112.
3.	*Vālmīki Rāmāyaṇa*	*Ayodhyā Kāṇḍa*-*Sarga*-100, *Śloka*-68, *Uttara Kāṇḍa Prak-ṣipta*-5.48, *Yuddha-kāṇḍa*-105.13.	*Ayodhyā*-76. 12, 13, 17, 18 *Ṛgveda*-U.K. P.-5.13, 32.	*Yajur-veda Kiṣkin-dhā* 35. 14.	*Sāmāni Sāmagāḥ Ayodhyā* 78.18
4.	*Mahā-bhārata*	*Trividhaṃ-Ādiparva*-1.48, 66, 207.9, *Trayī-vidyā Ādiparva*-100. 67, *Sabhā-Parva*-5.98, 38.	*Ādiparva*-3.56	—	*Dākṣiṇatya Pāṭha under* 207.9, *Sabhā parva*-11.30, 38.784, 80.8, 22, 23.

— The Middle Age (AD 1-1700 Approximately)

7	8	9
Uktha, Brahma Gāthā	*Atharvan, Bhṛgu, Aṅgiras*	*Atharvavedic Verse*
Veda, Kalpa-Sūtra, Vedāṅga-2.141, 4.98.	1.35, 59, 2.151, 3.198, 8.24.	Domination of Agriculture etc. — 10.82-84, 3.165, 4.5, 3.181, *Kṛtyāhananāni*-3.58, *Vaitāna Śānti-Karma*-7.78, *Viṣaghna-mantra-Maṇi*-7.217, 218, Projected under-8.350, *Āṅgīrasī Smṛti*-11.33, *Oṣadhī*-11.144.
3.4.114.	—	1.2.41-46, 1.5.101, *Kṛṣi-Vāṇijya-Pāśupālya-Vaṇik-Śilpa*-1.5.119, 120, *Śaṃnodevīstathā*-1.12.301, *Atharvāṅgirase*-1.13.313.
—	—	*Yuddhakāṇḍa*-12.2, *Bālakāṇḍa*-65.23, *Upavedas* of the *Atharvaveda-Bālakāṇḍa*-45.31, 1.14, 18.28, 37, *Ayodhyākāṇḍa*-1.29, 55.16, *Bālakāṇḍa*-15.2, 34.1, *Ayodhyākāṇḍa*-12.5, 25, 29, 36, *Araṇyakāṇḍa*-23.6, 25.5, *Sundarakāṇḍa*-5.15, *Yuddhakāṇḍa*-3.28
—	*Ādiparva*-2.194, 65.10, 66.4, 76.6, 77.2, 100.37, 120.52, 129.55, 131.71, 66.41, *Sabhā*-11.19.20.	*Vedaiḥ caturbhiḥ-Ādiparva*-1.20, 271, 2.382, 104.15, *Gāruḍa-Vidyā*-43.24, *Viṣanāśaka*-128.25, 58.24-26, 189.3, Agriculture-64.21, *Sabhāparva*-33.3, *Abhicāra-mantra-Ādiparva*-67.134, *Vaśīkaraṇa-mantra*-110.7, 121.12, 13. *Ādiparva*-70.37-40, 85.30-32, *Yātudhānī-Ādiparva*-154.11, *Brahmaveda Ādiparva*-155.5, *Lokaveda-Ādiparva*-161.6, *Vaitāna-vidhi-Ādiparva*-166.33, *Caturvaidya-Dākṣinātyapāṭha* under *Ādiparva*-206.25, *Sabhāparva*-12.47, Agriculture, Trade, Cattle feeding — *Sabhāparva*-5.77, 80, 115, 116, *Āyurveda-Sabhāparva*-5.91, 11.25, *Ṛṣi Kṛṣīvala-Sabhāparva*- 7.13, 11.32, 33, *Kauśika-Sabhāparva*-31.61.

1	2	3	4	5	6
5.	Some *Purāṇas*	—	—	—	—
6.	Introduction of the commentary of Sāyaṇācārya on *Atharvaveda*	*Aitareya Brāhmaṇa* 5.32, *Satyāṣāḍha Śrauta Sūtra*-1.1.1. *Ṛgveda Saṁhitā*-10. 90.2, *Taittirīya-Brāhmaṇa*-3.12.9.1, 1.2.1.26, *Taittirīya Saṁhitā*-6.5.10.3. *Smṛti*.	—	—	—

7	8	9
—	—	*Skanda Purāṇa-Kamalālaya-Khaṇḍa.* *Viṣṇu Purāṇa*-3.3.22, 3.5.14. *Matsya Purāṇa-Adhyāya*-215. *Śloka*-7. *Śrī Narasiṃha Purāṇa-Adhyāya*-27. *Śloka*-2, 3.
—	—	*Vandana Śloka*-8, *Mangalācaraṇa*-10, Page-5, *Āśvalāyana*-8.13, *Gopatha Brāhmaṇa*-3.2, 2.16, 2.24, 3.2, *Aitareya Brāhmaṇa*-5.33, *Bṛhadāraṇyakopaniṣad*-4.4.10. *Nṛsiṃhapūrvatāpanīya-1, Muṇḍakopaniṣad*-1, *Skanda Purāṇa-Kamalālaya Khaṇḍa, Viṣṇu Purāṇa, Bhaṭṭācārya, Kāmandakīya, Matsya Purāṇa, Mārkaṇḍeya Purāṇa, Atharvapariśiṣṭa, Taittirīyāraṇyaka*-2.15, *Atharvaveda-bhāṣyabhūmikā*-Page 69, 71.

Appendix 3 : Subjectwise Contribution

1	2	3	4	5	6	7
Sr. No.	*Name of the Seer*	*Politics*	*Religion*	*The Universe, Five Elements, Knowledge, Philosophy*	*Agriculture, Trade, Cattle-breeding*	*Thoughts about Women*
1.	Atharvan	1.2, 21, 2. 29, 3.3, 4, 5, 30, 5.3, 6.2, 65, 66, 87, 88, 98, 125, 126, 128, 7.18, 85, 86, 94.	6.15, 36, 60, 7.46-49, 61, 71, 97, 105, 106, 8.106, 12.5, 18.1-4.	1.1, 2.34, 3.10 5.1, 2, 6.11, 19, 80, 7.1-7, 20, 87, 8.9, 10.7, 11.7, 15.1-18, 19.19.	3.15, 4.5, 6.50, 92, 124, 7.18, 73, 10.9, 12.1, 19.25	1.11, 27, 3. 18, 6.17, 81, 82, 110, 139, 7.35, 36, 81, 115, 10.3.
2.	Brahmā	7.23, 33, 16.4.	6.114, 19. 1, 42, 58, 68, 71.	1.32, 2.16, 4.6, 5.27, 7.21, 22, 66, 67, 11.1, 13.1-4, 19.40, 43, 51, 72.	3.14, 28, 4.2, 7.104, 9.4, 7, 19.69.	3.23, 5.25, 11.5, 19. 28-30.
3.	Aṅgiras.	Some *Sūktas* with Atharvan.	1.13, 2.35, 5.12.	4.11, 19.22.	4.11.	1.14.
4.	Bhṛgu	2.5, 7.84.	1.13, 7. 107.	3.13, 4.11, 14, 6.15, 123, 19.53.	4.11. (with Aṅgiras)	1.14. (with Aṅgiras)

of the *AV*-Seers

8	9	10	11	12	13	14
Physiology and Hygiene	*Hygiene of the Human-Mind*	*Day-to-day Life of the People*	*Defence*	*Feeding, Peace and Satisfaction of the Society*	*Thoughts on National Integrity*	*Literature*
1.3, 9, 23, 30, 4.4, 5. 28, 6.50, 72, 85, 90, 101, 109, 136-138, 140, 7.56, 74, 76, 116, 19.37, 38.	1.10, 2.7, 23, 5.7, 6. 37, 112, 113, 130, 131, 7.35, 78, 9.2.	2.13, 3.37, 4.34. 6.68, 7.72, 11.3, 16.1, 19.26.	3.1, 2, 4.3, 5.24, 6.3, 4, 6, 7, 40, 7.13, 70, 117, 16.1, 2, 19.14-16, 17, 18, 20.	3.16, 26, 27, 5.11, 6.38, 39, 78, 86, 7. 19, 46-49.	1.15, 3.8, 30. 4.30, 6.44, 73, 74, 89, 94, 7.38, 19.24.	7.79, 80, 12.1.
1.17, 22, 24, 2.17, 33, 3.51, 4.5, 6.41, 7.32, 53, 8.1, 2, 11. 5, 19.60, 61, 63, 65, 67, 70	1.31, 3.31, 4.31-33, 5.9, 6.26, 115, 8.1, 2, 16.3, 19.52.	3.12, 5.26, 6.71, 7.60, 9.6, 10, 11.5.	1.19, 2.15, 24.5.20, 21, 19.66.	1.26, 7.33, 103, 19.9.	6.54, 17.1, 19.41, 62.	19.21.
1.12, 25, 2.3, 3.7, 5.4, 6.9. 20, 22, 83. 95, 97, 7. 30, 9.8, 19.39.	6.43.45. 46, 7.77, 10.1, 19. 34, 35	6.84, 127, 7.50, 9.3.	6.43, 7.31, 51, 90, 8.8, 11.10, 19.27.	4.39, 6.48, 99.	6.42.	—
1.12, 25, 3.7, 5.4, 6.20, 22, 91, 95, 96, 7.30, 9.8, 12.2, 19. 32, 33, 39, 44, 45.	3.25, 6.43.	6.27-29, 127, 9.3.	7.31, 108, 110, 8.8, 11.10, 19.27.	3.24, 6.16, 99, 19.54, 55.	6.42.	7.54.

1	2	3	4	5	6	7
5.	Vasiṣṭha	1.29, 3.19, 20, 4.22, 19.10-12.	—	—	—	—
6.	Śaunaka	7.12.	—	—	—	—
7.	Vāmadeo	3.9, 7.57.	—	—	—	—
8.	Sunkṣepa	6.25.	—	—	—	—
9.	Uddālaka	3.29	—	—	—	—
10.	Vena	—	—	2.1, 4.1, 2.	—	—
11.	Medhātithī	—	—	7.25.29.	—	—
12.	Nārāyaṇa	—	—	3.6, 10.2, 19.6.	—	—
13.	Kutsa	—	—	10.8.	—	—
14.	Śāntāti	—	—	—	1.33, 6.22, 23.	—
15.	Sindhudweep	—	—	—	7.89.	—
16.	Śaunaka	—	—	—	2.30, 7.11, 82.	—
17.	Uparibabhṛvā	—	—	—	6.30, 7.75	—
18.	Jaṭikāyana	—	—	—	6.116.	—
19.	Mātṛnāmā	—	—	—	—	—
20.	Āyuskāma	—	—	—	—	—

8	9	10	11	12	13	14
—	—	—	—	—	—	—
—	—	—	—	—	—	—
—	—	—	—	—	—	—
—	—	—	—	—	—	—
—	—	—	—	—	—	—
—	—	—	—	—	—	—
—	—	—	—	—	—	—
—	—	—	—	—	—	—
—	—	—	—	—	—	—
—	—	—	—	—	—	—
—	—	—	—	—	—	—
—	—	—	—	—	—	—
—	—	—	—	—	—	—
—	—	—	—	—	—	—
4.20, 8.6.	—	—	—	—	—	—
6.105.	—	—	—	—	—	—

1 2	3	4	5	6	7
21. Ṛbhū	—	—	—	—	—
22. Babṛu-pingla	—	—	—	—	—
23. Garut-mān	—	—	—	—	—
24. Bāda-rāyaṇi	—	—	—	—	—
25. Cātāna	—	—	—	—	—
26. Kāṇva	—	—	—	—	—
27. Śau-naka	—	—	—	—	—
28. Pramo-cana	—	—	—	—	—
29. Āgastya	—	—	—	—	—
30. Kau-śika	—	—	—	—	—
31. Śān-tāti	—	—	—	—	—
32. Prajā-pati	—	—	—	—	—
33. Śukra	—	—	—	—	—
34. Cātana	—	—	—	—	—
35. Kaban-dha	—	—	—	—	—

8	9	10	11	12	13	14
4.12.	—	—	—	—	—	—
6.14	—	—	—	—	—	—
4.6, 7, 5.13, 6.12, 100, 7.88, 10.4	—	—	—	—	—	—
4.37.	—	—	—	—	—	—
5.26, 6.32.						
2.31, 32, 5.23.	—	—	—	—	—	—
—	—	2.30.	—	—	—	—
—	—	6.106.	—	—	—	—
—	—	6.133.	—	—	—	—
—	—	6.117-119.	—	—	—	
—	—	—	6.107.	—	—	—
—	—	—	19.46.	—	—	—
—	—	—	4.40, 6.53, 134, 135, 8.5.	—	—	—
—	—	—	1.7, 16, 128 2.18, 4.36, 6.34, 8.3, 4.	—	—	—
—	—	—	6.75.	—	—	—

1	2	3	4	5	6	7
36.	Ācchośana	—	—	—	—	—
37.	Praśocana	—	—	—	—	—
38.	Śāmtāti	—	—	—	—	—
39.	Mṛgāra	—	—	—	—	—
40.	Śukra	—	—	—	—	—
41.	Viśvāmitra	—	—	—	—	—
42.	Yama	—	—	—	—	—
43.	Viśvāmitra	—	—	—	3.17, 5.36, 6.44.	—
44.	Gārgya	—	—	—	6.49, 19.7, 8.	—
45.	Kāṅkāyana	—	—	—	6.70	—

8	9	10	11	12	13	14
—	—	—	6.103	—	—	—
—	—	—	6.104	—	—	—
—	6.93, 11.6	—	—	—	—	—
—	4.23 to 28	—	—	—	—	—
—	2.11, 5. 14, 31.	—	—	—	—	—
—	5.15.	—	—	—	—	—
—	7.64, 100, 101, 16.5-9, 19.56, 57.					
—	—	—	—	—	—	—
—	—	—	—	—	—	—
—	—	—	—	—	—	—

Appendix 4 : India In the Atharvavedic Time — Some Rivers, Regions and Tribes

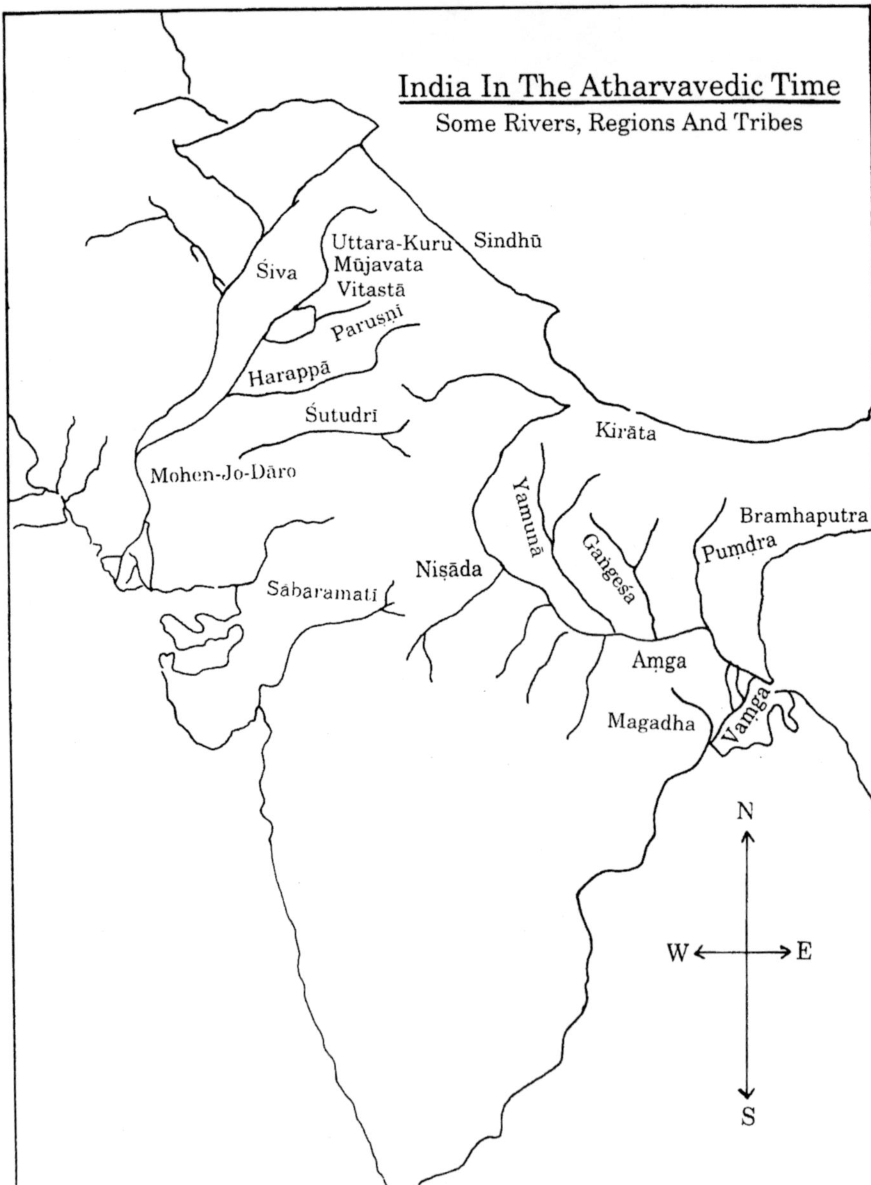

Not to scale

Bibliography

DICTIONARIES

Gīrvāṇa Laghukośa, Sanskrit-Marāṭhī, *Sampādak*, Janardan Vinayak Oka, M.A. Lokashikshan Karyalaya, Pune, Shake 1837.

(Principal) Vaman Shivaram Apte's *The Practical Sanskrit-English Dictionary* I, II, III. Editors P.K. Gode & C.G. Karve, Prasad Prakashan Poona, Revised Edition, 1957.

Molesworth's Marāṭhī-English Dictionary, Corrected Reprint, Shubhada Sarasvat, Poona, 1975.

ENGLISH

Absorption of Vrātyas, H.P. Shastri.

A Geography of Population, R.C. Candra.

A Historical Study of the Terms, Hīnayāna and Mahāyāna, R. Kimura, Calcutta, 1927.

A History of Indian Literature, Weber, London, 1892.

A History of Sanskrit Literature, K.B. Keith, Oxford, 1928.

Aitareya-Brāhmaṇa, ed. by K.S. Agashe, ASS, Poona, 1896.

Ancient Indian Historical Tradition, F.E. Pargiter, London, 1922.

An Introduction to the Study of Indian History, Prof. D.D. Kosambi, Bombay, 1956.

Āryan Invasion — A Myth, Dr. N.R. Waradpande, 1989.

Āsura India, Banarji Shastri Ananta Prasad, Patna, 1926.

Ayāramga Suttam, ed. by Jacobi.

Basic Ecology, Eugene P. Odum.

Bride-Wealth and Dowry, Goody-Jack and Stanlay, J. Tambiah Cambridge University Press, 1973.

Coins of Ancient India, Cunningham, A.

Collected Works, 4 Volumes of Prof. R.D. Bhandarkar.

Commemoration Volumes referred to in 'The Vrātyas in Ancient India' by Prof. Radhakrishana Caudhary, Caukhamba Sanskrit Series, Varanasi, First Edition, 1964, pp. 190, 191.

Der Vrātyā, Hauer J. Sttutgart, 1927.

Elements of Ecology, Brij Gopal, N. Bharadvaj.

Encyclopaedia of Environmental Science, Mc. Grow Hill.

Environmental Pollution and Health Hazards: Causes and Control, Ananda Gopal Mukharji.

Hellenism in Ancient India, G.N. Banarji.

Hindu Polity, K.P. Jayaswal, Bangalore, 1943-55.

Hindu-World, Volumes I & II by Benjamin Walkar, London, First Edition, 1968.

History of Indian Philosophy, S.N. Das Gupta.

Hymns of the Atharvaveda, Translated by Prof. R.T.H. Griffith, Vol. I, II — Munshiram Manoharlal, Reprint, 1885.

India as Known to Pāṇinī, V.S. Agarawal, Lucknow, 1983.

Introduction to Environmental Studies, Jonthan Jurk.

Jātaka, ed. by V. Fausbalt, London, 1877-87.

Journals referred to in *'The Vrātyas in Ancient India'* by Prof. Radhakrishna Caudhary, Caukhamba Sanskrit Series, Varanasi, First Edition, 1964, p. 191.

Kāśmīra Shaivism, J.C. Chatterji, Srinagar, 1914.

Kauśika-Sūtra: Dārila-bhāṣya, Tiḷaka Maharashtra Vidya-Peetha, Pune, First Edition, 1972.

Kavī and Kāvya in the Atharvaveda, Dr. N.J. Shende, University of Poona, First Edition, 1967.

Lāṭyāyana Śrauta-Sūtrā, BI, Calcutta, 1872.

Living Environment, Taylor Miller.

Lokāyata, D.P. Cattopadhyaya, Delhi, 1959.

Magadhan Literature, H.P. Shastri.

Magical Medicine, D. Hand-Wayland, Berkeley, Los Angeles, London, 1980.

Modern Concepts of Ecology, H.D. Kumar.

Plant Myths and Traditions in India, Gupta Shakti M. Leiden, Brill, 1971.

Position of Ruling Caste in Ancient India, *JOS* XIII-57, 376, E.W. Hopkins.

Religion and Philosophy of the Vedas and Upaniṣads, HOS, 2 Volumes, A.B. Keith.

Sacred Books of The East, Hymns from the Atharvaveda, M. Bloomfield, Oxford, 1897.

Sacred Books of The East, XXIX-XXX, H. Oldenberg, G. Bulher, Oxford, 1986-92.

Sacrifice in the Brāhmaṇa-Text, Prof. G.U. Thite, The Poona University Press, Poona, First Edition, March, 1975.

Some Women's Rites and Rights in the Vedas, Hanns Peter, Schmidt, BORI, Poona, 1987.

The Ātharvaṇic Civilisation, Karmbeḷkar, Nagpur, 1959.

The Atharvaveda and Gopatha-Brāhmaṇa, Maurice Bloomfield.

The Atharvaveda Saṁhitā, HOS, W.D. Whitney and C.R. Lanman, Cambridge, U.S.A., 1905.

The Fundamental Themes of The Atharvaveda, Prof. Durgamohan Bhattacarya, S.P. Mandaḷi, Tilak Road, Poona, 1967.

The Religion and Philosophy of the Atharvaveda, Dr. N.J. Shende, Reprint, 1952.

The Social Background of the Forms of Marriage in Ancient India, I-II, Chatterjee Heramba, Calcutta Sanskrit Pustak Bhandar, 1972-74.

The Vrātyas in Ancient India, Prof. Radhakrishna Caudhary, Caukhamba Sanskrit Series, Varanasi, First Edition, 1964.

Vedic Concepts of 'Field' and 'The Divine Fruitification', Dange Sadashiva Ambadas, Bombay, University of Bombay, 1971.

Village-life in Northern India, Lewis Oscar, Urban University, Illinois Press, 1958.

Voice of the Vedas, Dr. Suryakanta, published by S.P. Mandali, Tilak Road, Poona, 1969.

HINDĪ

Āpastamba Dharmasūtram, prakashak Jayakrishnadas Haridas Gupta, Caukhamba Sanskrit Series, Varanasi, Sana, 1932.

Atharvavedakā Subodha-bhāṣya-Prathama, Dvitīya, Tṛtīya Aura Caturtha Bhāga, Bhāṣyakāra, Padmabhooshana Dr. S.D. Satavaḷekar, Svadhyaya-maṇḍala, Pardi, Dist. Balasad, 1985.

Bhāradvāja Gṛhyasūtram, sampādak Henret J.W. Salomans, D. Lit. Ledan, 1913, Late E.J. Brill Limited, Motilal Banarsidass, Panjab Sanskrit Book-Depot, Sedamitha, Lahore.

Bodhāyana-Gṛhyasūtram, sampādak R. Shyamshastri, Government Branch Press Mysore, Dvitīyāvṛtti, 1920.

Drāhyāyana-Śrauta-sūtram, sampādak Brahmshri Mathuram, Mm. Ramanath Deexit, Madras 18, Prathamāvṛtti, 1982.

Gopatha Brāhmaṇa-bhāṣyam (Pūrvabhāga, Uttarabhāga), Pandit Kshemakaranadas Trivedi, *sampādak* Acarya Prajñadevi, Vyakaranacarya Medhadevi, Caukhamba Vidya-Bhavan, Post-box No. 669, Dvitīyāvṛtti, 1977.

Kātyāyana-Śrautasūtram — Bhāga 1, sampādak Mm. Pt. Nityanand Parvatiya, Caukhamba Sanskrit Series, Banaras, 1985. *Bhāga 2, sampādak* Dr. Mandanamishra Pracarya, Shri Lal Bahadur Shastri Sanskrit Vidyapeetha, New Delhi, Prathamāvṛtti, 1982, 83.

Manu-Smṛtiḥ, Pandit Haragovinda Shastri, Caukhamba Sanskrit Series, Varanasi, Dvitīyāvṛtti, 1965.

Ṛkvedakā Subodha Bhāṣya Bhāga 1-4, Pandit S.D. Satavaḷekar, Edition 2, 1983.

Sāmaveda, Pandit S.D. Satavaḷekar, Svadhyaya-Mandala Pardi, Available-1989.

Sāmavedīya Jaiminīya Upaniṣad-brāhmaṇam, Pandit Ramadeo, Shri Aurtail, Dayananda Mahavidyalay Sanskrit Granthamala-3, Lahore, 1921.

Sāmavedīya Tāṇḍya Mahā-brāhmaṇa Bhāga 1 va 2, sampādak Anandacandra Vedant Vageesh, Prathamāvṛtti, Calcutta, 1870.

Sāyaṇa-bhāṣyasahitā Atharvaveda Saṃhitā, Vyākhyākāra Sampādak, Ramasvaroop Sharma Gauda, Caukhamba Vidya-Bhavan Prakashan, Varanasi, Punarmudran Samskarana, 1990.

Śrīmanmaharṣī Vedavyāsapraṇīta Mahābhārata, Prathama khaṇḍa Ādi aura Sabhā-parva, Geeta Press, Gorakhpur, Caturtha Samskarna, Samvat-2030.

Śukla-Yajurvedīya Mādhyandina Śākhīyam Śatapatha-brāhmaṇam, Caukhamba Sanskrit Series, 1950.

Upaniṣat Saṃgraha Bhāga 1 va 2, sampādak, Pandit Jagadeesh Shastri, Motilal Banarsidas, Banglow Road, Jawahar Nagar, Delhi, Prathamāvṛtti, 1970.

Vaitāna-Śrautasūtraṃ Somāditya-Kṛtā Kṣepānuvidhi Saṃjñaka Bhāṣyopetam, sampādak Vishvabandhu Bheemadeo Pitambaradatta Vishveswarananda Samsthana, Hoshiyarpur, Punjab, Prathamāvṛtti, 1967.

Vājasaneyi Mādhyandina Śuklayajurveda, Pandit S.D. Satavalekar Pardi.

Vārāha-Gṛhyasūtrā, sampādak R. Shamashastri, Central Library, Baroda, 1921.

MARĀṬHĪ

Ādibhārat, Shripad Amṛt Dange, Tṛtīya āvṛtti, 1954.

Ādivāsiṃce Sāmājik Jīvana, Dr. Vilas Sangave, Pahili āvṛtti, 1972.

Aitareya Āraṇyakam, Ve. Sha. Saṃ. R.R. Babashastri Phadake, Anandashram Mudranalaya, Grantha 38, Pune, 1898.

Āpastaṃbīya Gṛhyasūtram, sampādak Dr. M. Winternitz, Vienna, 1887.

Āśwalāyana Gṛhyasūtram, Vedacarya, Vinayak Sharma Ghaisas, Ghaisas Guruji Vedapathashala, Pune, Shake 1907.

Āśwalāyana Śrauta Sūtram, Vedacarya, Vinayak Sharma Ghaisas, Ghaisas Guruji Vedapathashala, Pune, Shake 1907.

Atharvaveda — Sāyaṇabhāṣya Upodghāta, Late Pandit S.V. Pandit.

Atharvavedāce Marāṭhī Bhāṣāntara, Pandit Siddhesvara Shastri Citrav.

Bhāṃgaturā, Dr. Sarojini Babar, Maharashtra Rajya Sahitya Saṃskṛti-Maṇḍala, Muṃbai, Prathamāvṛtti, June, 1983.

Bhāradwāja Śrautasūtram, sampādak Prof. C.G. Kashikar, Vaidik Saṃshodhan Maṇḍala, Pune, Prathamāvṛtti, 1964.

Bhāratācā Śodha, Pandit Jawaharlal Nehru, *anuvādak* Sane-Guruji, N.V. Karandikar, Continental International Prakashan, Pune, Prathamāvṛtti, 1976.

Bhāratavarṣīya Prācīna Caritrakoṣa, Vidyanidhi Sidheswara Shastri Citrav, Prathamāvṛtti, 1932, Pune.

Bhāratīya Saṃskṛtikoṣa, sampādak Pandit Mahadeoshastri Joshi.

Bhāratīya Tattvajñāna Vaicārika Āṇi Sāmājika Saṃgharṣa, Dr. S.G. Saradesai, Lokavaṅmaya-gṛha, Mumbai.

Chandaḥ-Śāstram-Pingalācārya Viracitam, sampādak Pandit Kedarnath, Mm. Vasudeo Laxmanshastri Panashikar, Nirnayasagar Press, Mumbai, 1908.

Dās-Śūdrāṃcī Gulāmagirī Bhāga 1, Com. Sharad Patil, Prathamāvṛtti, 1982.

Dās-Śūdrāṃcī Gulāmagirī Bhāga 2, Com. Sharad Patil, Prathamāvṛtti, 1987.

Gautama-Praṇīta Dharmasūtrāṇi Haradattakṛta Mitākṣarā-Vṛtti Sahitāni, Ānandāśrama Sanskrit-granthāvaliḥ-Kramāṅka-61, sampādak Ve. Sha. Saṃ. Ganeshashastri Gokhale, Anandashrama Mudranalaya, Pune, Dvitīyāvṛtti, 1931.

Gāvagāḍā, Shri T.N. Atre, Tṛtīyāvṛtti, 1959.

Gāvagādyā-bāher, Dr. Prabhakar Mande, Parimala Prakashan, Aurangabad, Prathamāvṛtti, 1983.

Ghāṭāvarīla Śramikāṃcī Lokagīte, Mrs. Anasuya Limaye, Pune, Vidyapeetha Prakashan, Pune, Dvitīyāvṛtti, 1970.

Gulāmagirī, Mahatma Jyotiba Phule, Prakashak Gavaḷi Parishram Mudranalaya, Sevashram Vardha, 1990.

Hiṃdu-Saṃskṛtī Āṇi Strī, Dr. A.H. Saḷunkhe, Stri Uvaca, Prathamāvṛtti, 1989.

Khādira Gṛhyasūtram, sampādak, A. Mahadeoshastri, B.A.L. Shrinivasacarya Pandita, Government Branch Press, Mysore, 1913.

Kṛṣṇayajurvedīyam Taittirīyāraṇyakam — Bhāga 1, Ve. Sha. Saṃ. R.R. Babashastri Phadake, Anandashrama Mudranalaya, Pune, Sana 1897. *Bhāga 2*, Mm. Prof. Kashinatha Vasudeoshastri Abhyaṃkara, Anandashrama Mudranalaya, Pune, Sana 1969.

Loka-Sāhitya Āṇi Loka-saṃskrṛti-Saṃmelana, May 1961, Dr. Sarojini Babar, Maharashtra Sarakar Prakashan Vibhag, May 1961.

Loka-Sāhitya Eka Svatantra Abhyāsakṣetra, Prof. Dr. Gangadhar Narayan Morje-Dastane Ramchandra Ani Company, Pune, Prathamāvṛtti 1985.

Mahārāṣṭrātīla Jātisaṃsthāviṣayaka Vicāra, sampādak Prof. Yashawant Sumant, Dr. Dattatreya Pande, Pratima Prakashan Pune, Prathāmavṛtti, 1988.

Mahārāṣṭra Lokasaṃskṛtī Va Sāhitya, Dr. Sarojini Babar, National Book Trust, India, New Delhi, 1983.

Mahārāṣṭrīya Jñānakoṣa-Prastāvanā Khaṇḍa-Vibhāga Dusarā-Vedavidyā, Maharashtriya Jñanakoshamandala Limited, Nagapur, Tarphe-Shridhara Vyankatesh Ketakar, 481, Shanivar Peth, Pune, 1921.

Marāṭhī Viśvakośa, Khaṇḍa 1, Tarkateertha Laxmanshastri Joshi, Vishvakoshamaṇḍala, Wai.

Mārkaṇḍeya Purāṇa, sampādak Kashinath Vaman Lele, Shrikrishna Mudranalaya, Wai.

Matsya Purāṇa, Anandashrama Sanskritgranthavali, Pune, 1981.

Niruktam, Mudrak, Kshemaraja Shrikrishanadas Shresthi, Shrivyankteshvara (Steem) Mudranalaya, Khetawadi, Satavi Galli, Khambata Lena, Mumbai, 1969.

Pāraskara-Gṛhyasūtram, sampādak Mahadeo Gangadhara Bakre, Gujarathi Mudranalaya, Sasun-building, Circle Fort, Mumbai, Sana 1917.

Paryāvaraṇa-Śāstra, Dr. Prabhakar Karmakar, Ravikanta Pagnis, Vṛshali Devasthaḷi, H.K. Doiphode, Continental Prakashan, Pune, Dvitīyāvṛtti, 1989.

Pavāḍe-Bhāga 2, Shahira Khadilkar-Candrabhushan Prakashan, Mumbai, 16.

Prācīna-Bhāratīya Samāja Saṃskṛti Saṃvardhana Aitihāsika Rūpareṣā, Prof. D.D. Kosambi, Nivedaka, Ad. Jayant Gadkari, Granthali Prakashana.

Purāṇakathā Āṇi Vāstavatā, Dr. D.D. Kosambi, Bharatiya Itihas Shaṃshodhan Paddhati Pariṣad, Prathamāvṛtti, April, 1977.

Śāhīra, Shahira Annabhau Sathe, Abhinava Prakashan, Mumbai, Dusarī āvṛtti, August, 1985.

Sāmavedīya Jaiminīya Brāhmaṇa, Prof. Dr. Raghuveera, Dr. Lokeshcandra, Bhaga 31, Sarasvati Vihar, Nagpur, 1954.

Śaṃkhāyana Āraṇyakam, sampādak Vinayak Ganesh Apate, Grantha-90, Anandashrama Sanskrit-granthavali, Pune, 1922.

Saṃskṛti-Sugaṃdha, Dastane Ramchandra Aṇi Company, Pune-2. Dvitīyāvṛtti, 1977.

Śikṣādi Vedāṅga-Catuṣṭayam, sampādak Mm. Vasudeosharma Laxmanshastri Panashikar, Nirnayasagar Press, Mumbai, 1909.

Skanda Purāṇa: Kamalālayakhaṇḍa, Hastalikhita, Dharmakosha-maṇḍaḷa, Wai.

Śloka-Vārtika, Kumarila Bhatta, Ratna Publication, Prathamāvṛtti, 1978.

Śrīmad Vālmīki Rāmāyaṇam — Dākṣiṇātyapāṭha Śrī Rāmakośāvṛtti, sampādak Amarendra Laxman Gadagiḷa, Shri Ramakośamandala 1194, Sadashiv Peth, Pune, Prathamāvṛtti, 1982.

Śrī Vāsiṣṭha Dharmaśāstram, sampādak Reverent Lewis Anthon Bulhar, Balley, Āvṛtti-3, BIOR, Pune, 1930.

Śrī Yājñavalkya Smṛtiḥ — Mitākṣarāsaha-Bhashantarakar, Ve. Sha. Saṃ. R.R. Vishnushastri Bapat, prakashak R.R. Shankar Narhar Joshi, Citrashala Press, 1026, Sadashiva Peth, Pune, 1929.

Taittirīya Brāhmaṇa, Anandashrama Prakashan, Dvitīyāvṛtti, 1934.

Vaidika Saṃskṛtīcā Vikāsa, Tarkateertha Laxmanshastri Joshi, Prajña-pathashala-maṇḍala, Wai. Dusarī āvṛtti, 1972.

Vaidika-Yajña Madhyayugīna Tantrasādhanā Jñāneśvara-praṇīta Bhaktiyoga, Dr. S.R' Gadagiḷa, Dastane Ramchandra Ani Company, Pune, Prathamāvṛtti, 1979.

Vayyākaraṇa Siddhānta-Kaumudī, sampādak Krishnashastri Ramachandra Navare, Nirnayasagar Granthalaya, Mumbai, Cauthī Āvṛtti, Sana 1894.

Viṣṇu Purāṇa, Citrashala Press, Pune.

Index